Information Systems Development: Methods in Action

Information Systems Development: Methods in Action

Brian Fitzgerald, Nancy L. Russo and Erik Stolterman

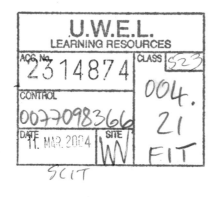

THE McGRAW-HILL COMPANIES

London · Burr Ridge IL · New York · St Louis · San Francisco · Auckland
Bogotá · Caracas · Lisbon · Madrid · Mexico · Milan
Montreal · New Delhi · Panama · Paris · San Juan · São Paulo
Singapore · Sydney · Tokyo · Toronto

Information Systems Development: Methods in Action
Brian Fitzgerald, Nancy L. Russo and Erik Stolterman
ISBN: 007709836 6

Published by McGraw-Hill Education

Shoppenhangers Road
Maidenhead
Berkshire
SL6 2QL
Telephone: 44 (0) 1628 502 500
Fax: 44 (0) 1628 770 224
Website: www.mcgraw-hill.co.uk

British Library Cataloguing in Publication Data
A catalogue record for this book is available from the British Library

Library of Congress Cataloging in Publication Data
The Library of Congress data for this book has been applied for from the
Library of Congress

Acquisitions Editor:	Conor Graham
Editorial Assistant:	Paul Von Kesmark
Senior Marketing Manager:	Jacqueline Harbor
Senior Production Manager:	Max Elvey

Produced for McGraw-Hill by Steven Gardiner Ltd
Text design by Steven Gardiner Ltd
Cover design by Hybert Design
Printed and bound in Great Britain by Bell and Bain Ltd, Glasgow

Contents

Preface

INTRODUCTION

Information systems development (ISD) has long been acknowledged as the core topic in the IS field, albeit one which has been very problematic. This is illustrated in the unacceptably large number of expensive high-profile IS failures, many of which have been well documented—even in the popular press—the London Ambulance computer-aided dispatch system and the Taurus stock exchange system, for example. However, even in the more routine ISD projects, the *vast majority* of projects exceed the expected development budget and schedule, and fail to adequately meet user requirements. These problems remain unsolved. Indeed, if anything the problems are likely to be further exacerbated due to the fact that the systems which need to be developed at present are increasing in complexity.

In recent times, the focus of IS research has shifted somewhat, as researchers have pursued more attractive but perhaps more ephemeral topics—business process reengineering, knowledge management, e-commerce come to mind. The purpose of this book is to aggregate and disseminate our views regarding the continuing importance of information systems development in current practice.

There are some signs of maturity in relation to ISD, however. For example, it is now widely accepted that ISD is not a solely technical challenge. Thus, it is no longer seen as just the technological transfer of a set of systems development techniques to "the great unwashed masses of IS developers" (as practitioners have been unfairly characterised in some academic quarters). Likewise, the challenge of ISD should not be seen as involving the straightforward application of one of the many commercial ISD methods which are so eagerly promoted by vendors and consultants. Rather, the importance of ISD contextual factors, and accommodation of both social and technical factors is now fairly widely accepted as essential. That is, success in ISD is not determined by which ISD method is used, nor by how well the analysis and design techniques are applied. Rather, the myriad of contextual factors that surround the enactment of the ISD development process—*the method-in-action*—are what primarily determine the outcome of the development.

This maturation and progression of thinking in relation to ISD is resonant with Gregory Bateson's (1972) distinction between first, second and third-order learning. In this progression, first-order learning is concerned with learning something directly. In relation to ISD, an example of first-order learning would be learning how to apply a technique such as entity relationship modelling or data flow diagramming. Moving to second-order learning, the focus becomes one of learning about learning. In the case of ISD, this might concern the selection and application of a commercial ISD method within which a range of ISD techniques might be incorporated. Third-order learning moves to a higher level again, one where the fundamental assumptions of what constitutes learning are considered. In relation to ISD, this would require understanding the myriad of factors which are relevant to the ISD context, and the effect they have on the development outcome. We believe that the state of ISD practice and ISD research have both advanced to the stage where third-order learning is appropriate, and that is what we would like to achieve with this book. Which brings us to the question of to whom this book is relevant.

WHO SHOULD READ THIS BOOK

We believe that this book will be useful reading for both practitioners and researchers. Taking practitioners first, we, as authors, have many years of hands-on ISD experience. This has been gained in a wide range of industry sectors in a number of countries world-wide. As a result, we genuinely believe that IS developers will find the material useful since it discusses the individual techniques and methods that comprise development, and also locates them in the overall ISD context. Management both within the IS function and also user management in general should find the material useful as well. The framework provided in the book indicates the relationship between the important components in ISD. Also, the framework can be used to represent a number of ISD scenarios which are frequently encountered in practice. However, in addition, the framework is also used to analyse and discuss recent trends in ISD such as ERP systems development and Open Source Software.

Turning to the academic audience, we have studied information systems development and method use in practice over many years, through large-scale surveys, longitudinal case studies, in-depth interviews, action research, and participation in systems development in Europe, Scandinavia, and the United States. The focus on method-in-action allows us to address issues related to how methods are truly used in practice. Thus, we believe the book will be useful to all IS researchers. It aims to provide 'the big picture' in relation to ISD. The framework may be used to locate a wide range of IS research. For this reason, MBA students or other graduate research students will find it a 'one-stop' reference in relation to ISD and recent trends in ISD. Also, undergraduate students, both those pursuing IS or Computer Science, or even those studying more general business courses will find the book provides a useful roadmap of significant aspects of ISD.

The text is not meant to be prescriptive, but to open readers' minds and cause them to reflect on the process and practice of information systems development. We hope you enjoy it!

HOW THE BOOK IS ORGANISED

Whereas there are a number of texts that do an excellent job of describing information systems development in general or of explaining one or more development methods or approaches in detail, we believe that this book is unique in its focus on the broader context of ISD. The book is built around a framework which integrates the various components of the ISD process—the developers (including users and other stakeholders), the information system itself, the development context, formalised methods, the roles played by methods, and the method-in-action.

In relation to the specific chapters which comprise the book, Chapter 1, sets the stage for the book. In this introductory chapter, we seek to make clear our understanding of ISD methods and their role in information systems development. To aid in the understanding of our view of methods, this chapter provides a definition of relevant terms.

Chapter 2, *A Framework for Information Systems Development*, presents the framework which we constructed to investigate the complex nature of IS development and the use of ISD methods in practice. The framework and each of its components are briefly described in this chapter. Subsequent chapters build on each of the components in more detail.

Chapter 3, *The Emergence and Evolution of Information Systems Development Methods*, provides a historical perspective on ISD in general, and ISD methods in particular. Such a perspective, by providing some insight into the past of ISD and ISD methods, helps us understand where we are today, and where we might be moving in the future. This chapter looks at methods that follow the systems development life cycle (SDLC). These include structured (or process-driven) approaches, data-driven approaches, approaches that integrate the process and data perspectives, and object-oriented approaches.

Chapter 4, *The 'Radical' Approaches – The Evolution Continues*, extends the historical overview of ISD and ISD methods. The methods discussed in this chapter are those that do not necessarily follow the traditional system development life cycle (SDLC). Among the approaches considered are Rapid Application Development (RAD) and eXtreme Programming (XP). The chapter also discusses 'softer' ISD methods, software process improvement and the Capability Maturity Model. Whereas the latter is not a method in itself, it does impact the way that organisations develop systems. The two final sections of the chapter deal with ERP systems and Open Source Software respectively.

Chapter 5, *From Formalised Method to Method-in-Action: The Rational and Political Roles of Methods*, discusses the relationship between formalised methods and method-in-action, and how this is mediated by the roles that methods play. The chapter presents a set of arguments and pressures which support the use of ISD methods, and identifies a set of *rational roles* of method which formalised methods may play. As a counterpoint, however, the chapter also identifies some factors and pressures which question the value of formalised methods. A set of *covert political roles* which methods can play are also presented. These serve to influence the derivation of the method-in-action.

Chapter 6, *The Development Context*, situates the development context as the foundation of information systems development. The importance of an awareness and detailed understanding of the context is emphasised as a vital part of our framework. Some basic aspects of the context and also the relationship between context, technology, culture and change are discussed in this chapter. Also, various ISD change strategies are identified, including proactive versus reactive, problem-solving versus innovation, incremental versus radical, long-term versus short-term, high risk versus low risk.

Chapter 7, *Developers*, considers the role of the actual developers in IS development. In our framework, developers are accorded a central role, as it is an inescapable fact that it is people not methods who develop systems, and that methods are at best an organising mechanism that should support developers. Thus, the importance in the development process of developer-embodied factors is explicitly acknowledged. These are leveraged by the developer during development and are drawn upon by the developer to analyse the development context, uniquely enact the method-in-action, and develop the actual information processing system.

Chapter 8, *Information Processing Systems*, focuses on the outcome of the ISD process, namely the resulting information system. The chapter presents a number of ways an information system can be categorised, described and understood. We believe that an awareness of the richness and diversity of systems is important for information systems development. Some of the topics covered here include families of systems, systems and change, and systems-driven development. The relationship between the system and the other parts of the framework are also discussed.

Chapter 9, *The Framework-in-Action: Method Tailoring*, examines the issue of method tailoring in some detail. The related research streams of contingency factors and method engineering are discussed. The chapter focuses in-depth on method tailoring in a very formalised development environment in a particular high-profile software development organisation, a very large multi-national telecommunications company. From this case, we draw lessons on tailoring which should be applicable to other organisations world-wide. A dual level tailoring strategy is described, comprising a macro level tailoring of components at the industry and organisational level, and micro level tailoring process at the individual project level.

Chapter 10, *The Framework-in-Action: Challenges to ISD*, illustrates the nature of ISD practice in a number of current development scenarios. The scenarios discussed are *open source software development*, *ERP (enterprise resource planning) development*, and *web development*. These three scenarios are chosen because they represent new forms of practice that are becoming increasingly mainstream. At the same time these new scenarios challenge the common and traditional understandings of ISD. We believe that the analysis presented in this chapter illustrates the strength of the framework and its general applicability, and also reveals how the framework can serve as a tool for analysis and evaluation of new scenarios and approaches in ISD.

Chapter 11, *Conclusion*, reiterates our fundamental belief that despite the changes in technology and topics, ISD remains at the core of the IS field. The role of the framework is reprised, and the central importance of the method-in-action concept is reiterated. The vital importance of adopting such a focus in relation to teaching ISD is emphasised. Also, the necessity for a closer alignment of ISD research and practice is discussed.

ACKNOWLEDGEMENTS

There are many who deserve mention for the contribution they made to this book. They include those people who participated in our research into the topic; the students who endured our lectures; the many academic colleagues who listened to our presentations, read our papers, and provided us with such excellent and thought-provoking feedback; the reviewers who recommended several useful amendments and additions; and not least, the many practitioner colleagues who sharpened considerably our thinking on the topic. There are undoubtedly errors in the book, and we must take responsibility for those ourselves. However, one of the bonuses of a co-authored book (along with the enormous fun we had in writing it) is that each of us can conveniently blame our co-authors for any errors!

Brian Fitzgerald, University of Limerick, Ireland
Nancy L. Russo, Northern Illinois University, USA
Erik Stolterman, Umeå University, Sweden

For our mothers, Wanzie, Norma and Gerd.

We must lie down where all the ladders start,
In the foul rag-and-bone shop of the 'art.
(Adapted from W.B. Yeats *The Circus Animals' Desertion*)

1

Introduction to IS Development

1.1 INTRODUCTION

Information systems abound in society today. These systems are generally made possible by the use of information technology, and have been developed for an almost infinite number of purposes. A fundamental principle—which may seem obvious but is nevertheless not always stated—is that all these systems have to be developed, and further, that someone must assume responsibility for doing that. Identifying the purpose, functions, structure and aesthetics of these systems is an extremely complex process. This book is about that process and how it can be approached in a methodical way.

We believe that *information systems development (ISD) is at the core of the IS field.* An analysis of the emergence of the field would certainly support this view. The major impetus behind the initial coalescing of the field of Information Systems was the fact that purely technical approaches to ISD did not successfully address the fundamental problems in information systems development; namely, that systems took too long to develop, cost too much to develop, and did not work very well in the context in which they were eventually deployed.

Information systems development is the fundamental process performed when engaging information technology to achieve a specific purpose in a specific context, although it involves much more than simply the deployment of technology. It is an activity that is fundamental in that it is stable over time even though the context in which it is performed changes. For example, it is well known that technology evolves and forces us to re-think our understanding of how it can be used. The ways in which organisations organise themselves have also radically changed over the last twenty years, and the manner in which information systems are used in these organisations has evolved. New fields of application have also emerged, but the fundamental development process persists. The development of information systems is still, and will probably always be, a core process with its own essential set of activities.

While information systems development remains a core process and its primary activities and goals are the same, there have been some significant changes in the last 30 years or so. Today, information systems development is often about deploying complete solutions which may be purchased ready-made off-the-shelf. Alternatively, it may involve configuring ready-made components into systems, or using high-level computer programming tools to produce software products. One of the key premises of this book is that none of these opportunities make information systems development obsolete. The basic activities of ISD still have to be accomplished. The developer still has to investigate, analyse and design the system's purpose, function, structure, appearance, behaviour, cost and efficiency. And despite the changes in the field, all this has to be done in relation to how the system will fit a specific context and relate to other systems. So, even if some components in the design (such as software products) are more standardised or ready-made, other aspects (such as organisational structure, competence, speed of change) have increased the overall complexity. Regardless of pre-conditions, the *information system is a result of an intentional compositional process*. The system must be composed to fit resources, constraints, needs, wishes, and all the unique exigencies of the specific context.

Over the years, many attempts have been made to address these complex and difficult activities using a more formalised and methodical approach—the goal being to rationalise and better control both the development process and the outcome of that process. This book is about these attempts, their successes and failures, and their future. Information systems development can be approached in a number of ways. The theme of this book is *methods-in-action*. We have chosen to address the fundamental issues of information systems development from the perspective of practice. Nevertheless, we also have to focus considerable attention on the more conceptual and intellectual aspects that underpin this practice.

A fundamental 'component' of information systems development is that of the *developer*. We have chosen to use the term in a broad and inclusive sense. This is based on the realisation that systems are typically not developed by a single person with a clearly defined professional competence. An information system is the result of the thoughts and actions of a multiplicity of stakeholders, including system users, analysts, designers, programmers, clients, problem owners and decision makers. Usually the developer is to be understood as a team. These teams can range from the traditional small group of highly specialised professionals to teams consisting of a diverse and large number of actors. In the book we address this fact by using the notion of the *practitioner* or developer in a broad and inclusive way. Still, our main focus is on the professional developer, educated and trained to do information systems development work. It is important that the developer is accorded a central role in the field of information systems development, thus reflecting the fact that it is people, not methods, who develop systems.

The use of methods for information systems development has been the focus of much research over a long period of time. The major point of contention has been whether the methods available actually do help in the development process. In the early days, methods were developed to address inherent problems in the process, namely that systems were not developed on time, within budget, nor of good quality. However, even with the introduction of these methods, the aforementioned problems have not been eliminated. Plausible reasons for this failure have been identified, both in academic research, and also by practitioners. One of the main reasons proposed in the academic literature is that practitioners do not fully realise the need and the benefits of using the methods which have been promulgated by researchers (see Chapter 5). The practitioner complaint, on the other hand, has mainly been that the available methods do not fit the complexity of the development situations. Methods have almost been seen as non-relevant to practice, and are mainly used because they appear plausible. One practitioner, interviewed in the course of our own research into this topic, captured the spirit of this unquestioning adoption of ISD methods as follows:

We may be doing wrong, but we're doing so in the proper and customary manner.

In this book, we will try to find a common understanding of the relationship between information systems development and methods. We believe that such an understanding can be created by taking information systems development practice and method-in-action as the focal point of study. The purpose is not to come up with new or better methods. Instead we hope to present a way of understanding practice and a way of thinking about methods that will be both practical and congruent with many years of our research into method-in-action.

The purpose of this chapter is to set the stage for the readers of this book. We want to make clear our understanding of methods and their role in information systems development. We believe that it is essential to consider information systems development methods in the context in which they are used, rather than as abstract, isolated activities. To aid in the understanding of our view of methods, we begin with a definition of terms. This is then followed by two sections which discuss the contextual aspects of method-in-action.

1.2   DEFINITION OF TERMS

Arriving at precise and universally accepted definitions of terms is especially difficult in the information systems field, as researchers tend to use the same terms to denote different concepts, and different terms to denote the same concept, the perennial problem of homonyms and synonyms. We have chosen to provide definitions, or clarifications as to our usage at least, for several basic terms which are used throughout the book. These include *information system, information systems development v. software design, methodology v. method, development process model, technique* and *tool.* Many definitions exist in the literature for these basic terms, but there is by no means unanimous agreement as to what these terms mean or how they should be used. Even where researchers provide deliberate and explicit definitions, they vary in terms of rigour, between colloquial common-sense definitions, and those which are very conceptual and introduce much in the way of additional primitive terms.

For example, a wide variety of definitions for the term *information system* have been proposed. This multiplicity of definitions is considered by Verrijn-Stuart (1989) who proposes two broad categories of definitions:

> **Information systems in the broader sense**: defined as 'the totality of all formal and informal data representation and processing activities within an organisation, including the associated communication, both internally and with the outside world'.

> **Information systems in the narrower sense**: defined as 'computer-based sub-systems, intended to provide recording and supporting services for organisational operation and management'.

A definition which is in keeping with the broader definition just proposed, is that provided by Buckingham *et al.* (1987, cited in Avison & Fitzgerald, 1988, p. 8). They define an information system as:

> a system which assembles, stores, processes and delivers information relevant to an organisation (or to society), in such a way that the information is accessible and useful to those who wish to use it, including managers, staff, clients and citizens. An information system is a human activity (social) system which may or may not involve the use of computer systems.

However, although the use of computers may not be essential, it is nevertheless the case that Information Systems actually exists as a distinctive field of study because of its focus on computer technology. Notwithstanding this, we believe there is a need to recognise the information systems concept at a logical level (what it is) free of its physical form (how it is performed whether using a computer or not).

Another contentious issue concerns the word *methodology*. It has come to be used synonymously with *method* in much of the literature. However, several research-ers have striven to differentiate the methodology and method concepts (e.g. Avison & Fitzgerald, 1995; Checkland, 1981; Oliga, 1988; Vonk, 1990; Welke, 1983). Typically, this differentiation is premised on methodology being a higher-order construct than method, although some researchers actually reverse this, proposing method as encom-passing methodology (Davis, 1982; Hackathorn & Karimi, 1988).

Constantine (1989, p. 232) has provided a forthright explanation for the use of the term methodology rather than method:

> *The computer field likes big words ... A software design* method *sounds like the sort of generic-brand thinking that anyone could work out over a long weekend. But a software design* methodology *sounds like an elaborate and well-thought out concept, perhaps worth attending a seminar on by a major software guru.*

Despite this differentiation between the terms methodology and method, several researchers have criticised the use of the term methodology, as it actually means 'study of method'. Indeed, Stamper (1988) put the case quite forcibly:

> *I use the term 'methodology' under protest, bowing only to customary usage. It would be better, as in the philosophy of science, to speak of 'methods' when referring to specific ways of approaching and solving problems, and to reserve 'methodology' for comparative and critical study of methods in general; otherwise this vital field of study is nameless.*

Stamper's point is a valid one, since this nomenclature could lead to the logical, but obviously ludicrous, situation whereby research in the area of systems development methodology could be categorised as methodology*ology*. Thus, we believe the term 'method' is more straightforward and useful, and it is the term used in this book. An information systems development method may be defined as:

> *A coherent and systematic* approach, *based on a particular* philosophy *of systems development, which will guide developers on* what *steps to take,* how *these steps should be performed and* why *these steps are important in the development of an information system.*

Different estimates exist as to the number of commercial IS development methods available, from hundreds (Avison & Fitzgerald, 1995) to over a thousand (Jayaratna, 1994). We also use the term 'formalised method' in this book to refer to these commercial, brand-named methods, and also those methods which have been developed internally within an organisation, but which are formally documented. Formalised methods should not be confused, however, with formal methods, such as VDM or Z, which are methods that draw on mathematically-expressed formalisms as a basis for system specification and design.

There is more general consensus on a definition of *technique*. Whereas a method is concerned with 'what to do', a technique addresses more the 'how to do it' question. Also, in contrast to methods, techniques are generally non-proprietary and tend to be incorporated into many different methods. Thus, a method may involve techniques, but it is the method which determines if a particular technique is appropriate or not. Examples of techniques would include data flow diagrams (DFDs), entity relationship diagrams (ERDs), entity life histories (ELHs), state transition diagrams (STDs), use cases, joint requirements planning (JRP), and process specification techniques such as decision tables, decision trees, action diagrams, Nassi-Shneiderman diagrams, Structured English, Tight English, and pseudocode. Prototyping of user requirements could be classified as a technique. However, prototyping can also be classified as an approach to development, or as a systems development process model—an issue discussed below.

In line with this, a *tool* may be defined as an instrument which may be used in performing a technique. Thus, a technique may deal with the logical way of how to do an activity and is more to do with knowledge than a product. The tool, often computerised, is more tangible and may be used to help produce some deliverable which the method or technique requires. Examples of tools would include CASE (Computer Assisted Software Engineering) products such as a diagramming tool, an electronic data dictionary, and a test case harness.

There are other important concepts relevant to information systems development which have not been completely covered by the classification proposed thus far. Prototyping is one issue, as already mentioned. The systems development life cycle (SDLC) is another. Many tend to consider the SDLC as a method. However, while it is inextricably linked with methods, it lacks the characteristics that would satisfy the definition of method proposed above. The SDLC typically contains a series of development phases arranged in a certain sequence. It is certainly the case that each development project follows a systems development life-cycle, and the life-cycle concept is at the heart of many methods. However, it is not synonymous; rather it is a higher-order construct. Thus, an SDLC such as the waterfall model actually underpins many methods. Other approaches such as iterative development, incremental development, evolutionary development, prototyping, also fall into this category. The term we have chosen to represent this category is *development process model*. It is not unusual that a method is a combination of different development process models. A method might, for instance, be based on incremental development and on prototyping. These issues are discussed in more detail again in Chapters 3 and 4.

In this book, the term *information systems development* is used, rather than a term such as *software design*, for example. Again, these terms are often treated as synonymous in the literature. However, information systems development may be differentiated from software development in a technical environment in so far as the latter often requires mathematical sophistication, whereas information systems development relies more on communication and interaction skills. Software design has a narrower focus, and addresses issues such as the design of efficient algorithms, and the use of notations to document computational logic. Information systems development focuses on the systemic character of an information system – the information system in the organisation – in contrast to software design that brings the 'isolated' software in focus. Following from this, the term *developer* is also used rather than *designer* to represent the practitioner (analyst, programmer, engineer, end-user) who develops the information system.

1.3   THE SYSTEMIC ASPECT OF INFORMATION SYSTEMS DEVELOPMENT

Information systems are developed for a specific situation, in a specific organisation or company. We would not define a ready-made, off-the-shelf software product as an information system since it is a generic product aimed for a broad spectrum of use. Information systems development, on the other hand, is always relevant to a particular situation, and even to a specific system in a specific situation. The product is a unique system, typically encompassing not only software but also new work procedures and personnel roles. Ready-made, off-the-shelf software can be a component of a deployed information system. Yet even when an information system includes ready-made software, the activities of information systems development are performed to determine the system requirements and to adapt the product to fit the particular circumstances.

Today, most information systems are not only conceptually part of a larger system, but are connected to and interact with other systems, possibly in a global network. Information systems development is therefore not usually concerned with developing systems in contexts where none already exist. Instead, more importance is placed on how the 'new' system will fit within the inter-connected environment. Because of the prevalence of intra- and inter-organisational systems, the systemic aspect of the development process is more apparent today than in previous decades.

This systemic aspect also leads to a development process where knowledge about the context becomes increasingly important. To develop an information system means to add something new to an existing system or network of systems. The developer has to compose a wholeness out of the existing and the new; in other words, the new system must fit seamlessly with the other component systems. The resulting system will be judged on how well the overall composition is working, not solely on the properties of the new addition.

Information systems development is therefore a process demanding a very wide range of skills and knowledge. The systemic aspect of information systems renders the development process a very complex and diverse enterprise. Methods are one way of trying to make this complexity manageable. The question remains— how should we understand and use methods if we want them to provide real support for this complex development process?

1.4   METHODS AND RELATIONSHIPS

As mentioned above, information systems development is something that takes place in a complex web of relationships. The number of variables and factors that influence the process is potentially infinite, which means that the process may be overwhelming in its complexity. In our examination of the basic issues concerning information systems development, we will not be able to cover all aspects of this complex process. Our focus will be on developing an understanding of method-in-action, based on practice-based research findings. We have tried to investigate the richness and complexity, without being deluged in the detail, and we have chosen to focus our attention on just a few vital relationships.

One of the key relationships—the primary *raison d'etre* for this book, in fact, is *formalised method v. method-in-action*. Formalised methods have been promoted as capable of rendering the development process to be more efficient, more secure, more predictable and easier to control. However, the research literature suggests that these methods have not always been used, and, if used, not always in the way they were intended to be used. The tension between formalised methods and method-in-action is contentious in almost every development project in every organisation. This book is based on the assumption that better use of methods can be achieved through a more comprehensive understanding of this tension.

To the individual developer the most interesting and important relationship may be the *developer – method* interaction. The basic idea behind method use is to remove some responsibility from the developer. The method is supposed to help inform the developer as to what has to be done and how it can or should be done. The more that is prescribed by the method, the less that is left to the developer. The more freedom given to the developer, the less that is then possible to prescribe or control by means of the method. This tension is at the core of development practice and is recognised by practitioners.

In addition, all development takes place within the *context – method* relationship. It is possible to distinguish between two types of contexts: immediate and secondary. The immediate context is the specific situation for which an information system is being developed. The secondary context comprises the total organisational context within which the development process takes place. Any method will be used in a context with specific traditions and an established work culture. The culture and traditions of work are usually established over time, and are very difficult to change radically in a short time. This might be due to the fact that change is often considered dangerous and threatening. Any method brings about change to the development process – if not, there is no basis for using methods. Methods are supposed to change and, ideally, improve practice. Methods are used because the established work culture does not deliver results in a desirable fashion (whatever that might be). Methods are a way to change the environment in which they are deployed, but the environment is likely to be resistant to change.

These relationships cause conflict or tension within the development process. Whereas these tensions cannot be eliminated, a better understanding of their causes and effects can help developers manage these conflicts in the best way possible. Looking at the development process from this perspective and reflecting on the impact of the context, the method, and the developer's own experiences can assist the developer in identifying an appropriate approach for a particular development situation.

In Chapter 2, we develop a framework which seeks to capture the complex nature of IS development in practice. This chapter then forms the structure around which we build the rest of the book.

1.5   DISCUSSION QUESTIONS

1.   Identify a particular change that has occurred in the way organisations operate today and discuss the impact of this on the way information systems are used to support the organisation.

2.   Why are definitions of information systems and information systems development important?

3.   Consider formalised methods and procedures used in a field other than information systems. How are information systems development methods similar and how are they different? Why?

4.   You interact with information systems every day. Think about one of these systems, and identify the contextual factors that may have played a role in its development.

5.   If methods are not absolute guides for information system development, then why is it worthwhile to learn methods at all?

2

A Framework for Information Systems Development

2.1 INTRODUCTION

In this chapter we present a framework which we have derived to investigate the complex nature of IS development and the use of ISD methods in practice. The framework has been constructed on the basis of a detailed investigation of the ISD literature, and also incorporates the results of our empirical research which has investigated this topic in considerable depth (e.g. Fitzgerald, 1994; Fitzgerald, 1997; Fitzgerald, 1998; Fitzgerald & O'Kane, 1999; Fitzgerald, Russo & O'Kane, 2002; Russo & Wynekoop, 2000; Russo, Wynekoop & Walz, 1995; Stolterman, 1991; Stolterman, 1992). This empirical research has been conducted both in Europe and the US, and has involved several large scale surveys, in-depth interviews, and case studies in a large number of companies representing a wide range of industry sectors, including banking, software houses, multinationals in the pharmaceutical, food processing, public utility, telecommunications sectors, and also government agencies. Thus, it represents a wide cross-section of ISD practice in a variety of important contexts.

The framework and each of its components are briefly described in this chapter. Subsequent chapters build on each of the components in more detail.

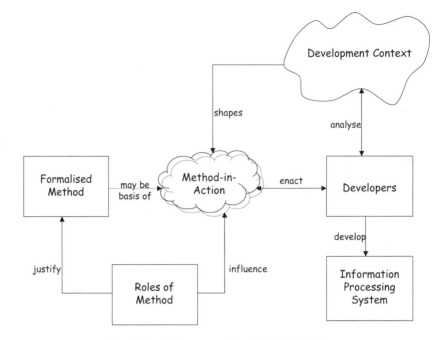

Fig. 2.1   A Framework for ISD Method Use

2.2   A FRAMEWORK FOR INFORMATION SYSTEMS DEVELOPMENT METHOD USE

Despite the abundance of conceptual and empirical research on ISD methods, there is no widely accepted framework for studying the use of these methods. This is all the more problematic given the fact that a huge number of methods exist, with estimates ranging from several hundred (Longworth, 1985; Avison & Fitzgerald, 1995) to over one thousand (Jayaratna, 1994). Some differ in fairly trivial aspects while others differ fundamentally, both in paradigm and in coverage. Thus, methods range from the 'hard' rationalistic ones that have a technical focus to 'soft' human-oriented ones with a social focus. Also, methods differ markedly in coverage—some do not address preliminary analysis phases, while others ignore later implementation activities. These issues are discussed in more detail in the next two chapters which consider the emergence and evolution of ISD methods.

Based on an extensive and detailed investigation of the literature on ISD and on our own empirical research into the topic, we constructed the framework which is presented in Fig. 2.1. Each of the components of the framework is explained briefly in the remaining sections of this chapter. Subsequent chapters elaborate the individual components in greater detail.

2.3   EXPLANATION OF THE FRAMEWORK

2.3.1   Formalised Method

Formalised methods are one of the traditional focal points in ISD research. As already mentioned, we intend the term formalised method to include formally documented in-house methods and commercially available ones. Examples of the more popular commercial methods include Information Engineering, Structured Systems Analysis and Design Method (SSADM), the Structured Approach, Soft Systems Method (SSM), Multiview, Dynamic Systems Development Method (DSDM). Formalised methods will be discussed in more detail in Chapters 3 and 4 which consider the emergence and evolution of formalised ISD methods. These formalised methods, whether commercial or in-house, are typically documented in several manuals. Formalised methods are sometimes embodied in software tools, such as CASE (Computer Assisted Software Engineering) tools or application development environments. This book will not specifically address these tools however, since within the approach to ISD that we adopt, these tools can actually be viewed as a type of formalised method.

2.3.2   Method-in-Action

In actual development practice, formalised ISD methods are rarely applied in their entirety, nor as originally intended by their creators, although they may provide a template to guide development practice. This is depicted in the framework in Fig. 2.1 by the dashed line which reflects the view that while some kind of method-in-action will be used, a formalised method *may* be the basis but is not essential. This distinction between an original formalised method and the method-in-action has parallels with the distinction drawn by Argyris & Schon (1974) between an 'espoused theory' and a 'theory-in-use'. Thus, methods are never applied exactly as originally intended. Different developers will not interpret and apply the same method in the same way; nor will the same developer apply the same method in the same way in different development situations. Therefore, on any development project, the method-in-action is uniquely *enacted* by the developer. This unique enactment for every development project is reflected in our framework in Fig 2.1 by the fuzzy, cloudy outlines. In subsequent sections, we will consider how the method-in-action is shaped by the development context, and how it is influenced by the roles of method. This progression from formalised method to method-in-action is discussed in detail in Chapter 5.

2.3.3   Roles of Method

An important component of the framework is that of the roles of method. This includes two broad, but diametrically opposed, categories of roles that methods can play in the development process. Firstly, there are a set of *rational roles* which form part of the conceptual basis and rationale behind the use of methods. For example, IS development is a very complex process, and methods help address this by providing a reductionist subdivision of this process into plausible and coherent steps. Also, by rendering the development task more visible and transparent, methods facilitate project management and control of the development process, thus reducing risk and uncertainty. Another related role that methods provide is that of a purposeful framework for the application of techniques (such as feasibility studies, steering committee reviews, etc.) and resources at appropriate times during the development process. There is also an economic role in that methods may allow skill specialisation and a division of labour in the ISD process (e.g. analysis, design, coding and testing). That is, by breaking the ISD process into these discrete activities, each of which can receive different remuneration rates, some economic savings become possible. Methods also play a role in providing a structural framework for the acquisition of knowledge. Thus, any learning from past development experiences can be systematised and stored for future reference. They also help standardise the development process, thus facilitating inter-changeability among developers. Also, methods can lead to increased productivity and quality, as the resources needed for development may be predicted more accurately, and made available as and when necessary.

However, there is also a set of *political roles* that methods may play. Again, these have been discovered through our empirical research. For example, ISD methods act as a 'comfort factor,' in that method use provides some reassurance that 'proper' practices are being followed, or provides confidence that development decisions have been made on a systematic basis. In a similar fashion, they may act as a 'legitimacy factor', whereby organisations claim to use a method to win contracts with government agencies, for example, or to help achieve ISO-certification. Methods may also help provide an audit trail of the development process to afford protection if ISD decisions turn out to be wrong in the future. Likewise, they contribute to 'professionalising' systems development work, thereby insulating developers from conceding to unreasonable deadlines and demands from user departments. Another political role they can play is to provide a 'power-base' for method champions who may use it to raise their profile within an organisation.

Issues to do with these rational and political roles of methods are discussed in more detail in Chapter 5.

2.3.4   Development Context

The framework acknowledges the complexity and dynamic nature of the business context in which development takes place. This is represented as a cloud shape in Fig. 2.1, reflecting the fact that development takes place in a unique real context, and this context cannot always be easily analysed to produce a neat and regular specification of user requirements. This unproblematic specification of user requirements is a fundamental expectation of the 'hard' engineering approaches to systems development (which will be discussed in Chapter 3). The essence of this expectation is well captured in McMenamin & Palmer's (1984, p. 77) contention that "the specification should contain all the true requirements and nothing but the true requirements." However, much research has indicated that identifying the "true requirements" may not be feasible practically (Stage, 1991), and indeed, there may also be limits to what should be known from a social and ethical point of view (Jones and Walsham, 1992).

Even if different development contexts are similar in some respects, a context is always unique. The specific situation within which development takes place and the finalised system will be implemented, creates unique preconditions for the development process. An awareness of that uniqueness is a foundation for all successful ISD projects.

Formalised methods usually prescribe how a development situation must be approached in a methodical way independent of the type of context. However, we do not accept this and contend that certain characteristics of the development context *shape* the method-in-action, as indicated by the arrow in Fig. 2.1. For example, the accelerating pace of change characteristic of the business environment facing organisations today is a common theme in contemporary research—"the faster metabolism of business today" as Rockart and De Long (1988) term it. This requires organisations to act more effectively in shorter timeframes, but formalised methods are typically oriented towards large-scale development with a long development time. In the climate of continuous change that organisations are now faced with, short-term needs dominate, and these in turn mean that the economics of formalised systems development is dwindling. Developers, thus, do not have the luxury of being able to patiently follow a comprehensive formalised method. Indeed, the truncation of some phases in the development process is probably inevitable, and this shapes the method-in-action.

The phenomenon of IS development backlogs in organisations is well documented. These are of two types—the visible backlog and the invisible backlog. The visible backlog refers to the systems which have been formally requested and are scheduled for eventual development. However, many users, despairing at the size of the visible backlog, do not request systems that that they may need, thus giving rise to an invisible backlog which has been estimated to be about three times larger than the visible backlog. Indeed, it has been suggested that a ten-fold increase in system development productivity is needed to address the current demand for ISD. Thus, many organisations have construed the issue as a productivity versus rigour one, and while rigour may be associated with patiently following the steps of a formalised method, the absolute need for productivity shapes the method-in-action which strives to improve productivity—with the latter seen as more important.

In recent times, we have witnessed a basic restructuring in the software industry whereby companies are relying far less on in-house development of systems, but are pursuing alternative strategies such as buying package software or outsourcing system development. One of the effects of this altered profile of development is that users are constructing their own information systems out of multiple packages, integrated together by specially written software which addresses their individual unique needs. This altered development profile further serves to shape the method-in-action, as most existing formalised methods do not address this mode of development.

These issues to do with the development context are discussed in detail in Chapter 6.

2.3.5   Developers

Another component of the framework is that of developers. The term is used in its broadest sense, however, and is intended to cover the multiplicity of stakeholders, system users, analysts, designers, programmers, clients and problem owners. It is extremely appropriate that the developer is accorded a central role in the framework, thus reflecting the fact that it is people, not methods, who develop systems. Methods are merely frameworks which must be leavened by the wisdom of human developers if they are to be effective. The ingenuity and ability of the developer cannot be abstracted to any formalised ISD method. However, the varied skill levels of different developers is not acknowledged in formalised methods. For example, one of the explicit goals of the Jackson Systems Development (JSD) method (see Chapter 3) is to eliminate personal creativity from the development process.

There are several strands of research in the literature which confirm the importance of developer factors. For example, huge variances in the capabilities of different developers and a consequent impact on development productivity have long been reported (Boehm, 1981; Brooks, 1987; Peters & Tripp, 1977). Also, the importance of learning over time as developers increase their level of expertise needs to be acknowledged, as does the significant contribution made by developer knowledge of the application problem domain or business context. These factors are important and are taken into account in the framework in the manner in which the developer *analyses* the development context and uniquely *enacts* the method-in-action to *develop* an information processing system.

The developer component and these issues are discussed in more detail in Chapter 7.

2.3.6   Information Processing System

At its heart, ISD is a socio-technical discipline. Both the social and the technical elements are equally important. Historically, the emphasis in the early years was on technical issues (see Chapter 3), with developers striving to become more engineering-like in their approach to development, as that was seen as having the potential to solve problems in the development process. However, it was quickly realised that information systems have a very strong social component, and in recent years the pendulum has swung to more emphasis on social issues. It is clearly the case that both social and technical elements are vital for ISD. While social factors are critically important, it is the technology that serves to uniquely characterise the field, and it is certainly a key aspect of the field in any lay-person's definition of it.

Just as the development context is not homogeneous, nowadays the information processing systems being developed are not all alike. A number of *families of systems* can be identified. A family of systems is a group of systems that have some similar characteristics. ISD is to a large extent based on the reuse of development patterns, as recognised by experienced developers. The family resemblance between systems makes it possible, despite the uniqueness of each system, to use knowledge from earlier development projects.

Families of systems can be typified, for instance, by dimensions such as the purpose of the system (entertainment, administration, education, communication, etc.), or the complexity of the system. Other characteristics possible to use in a classification are unique versus generic systems and solved versus unsolved problems. These different dimensions can be used to form a more general understanding of a system, even if it has to fit a unique context. These fundamental aspects of a system also influence the way it must be developed. For example, the development of a unique, highly complex system for education focused on an earlier unsolved problem of education is very different from the development of a general, not so complex, administrative system focused on a standard solved problem.

These families are therefore important, as the differing characteristics of each family serves to affect the method-in-action that will be needed to develop them. The information processing system component is discussed in more detail in Chapter 8.

2.4   CHAPTER SUMMARY

In this chapter, we presented a framework to illustrate the nature of IS development, and some significant aspects and factors that need to be considered, including the concept of method-in-action. The framework has been derived from intensive study of previous research on ISD, and also is informed by our own empirical research into the topic conducted over a long number of years. The framework is used to structure the remainder of the book.

An important aspect of the framework is its recognition of the complexity of ISD as a fully dynamic dialectic system in itself. Each component of the framework contributes to the overall system. At the same time the framework shows that it is never possible to comprehensively define any of the components without taking the whole framework into consideration. The framework is not itself a method; it does not prescribe action. Instead the framework makes it possible for practitioners and researchers to reflect on ISD as a rich and complex process influenced by all the framework components and their interactions.

The framework components were briefly introduced here, but each component is elaborated in more detail in subsequent chapters, beginning with a historical perspective on the emergence and evolution of ISD methods which is the focus of the next two chapters.

2.5   DISCUSSION QUESTIONS

1.   Consider the framework as a map of information systems development. What else could be included in the framework? Is there anything that could be omitted?

2.   Think about a particular development situation. Try to analyse it by using the framework.

3.   For whom might a framework such as the one presented in the chapter be valuable? And for what purposes?

4.   What might be the dangers with a framework that describes information systems development?

5.   One of the goals of the framework is that it should apply generally to the field of ISD. Is there a problem with being general? And what might the benefits be?

3

The Emergence and Evolution of Information Systems Development Methods

3.1 INTRODUCTION

The purpose of this chapter and the next one is to provide a historical perspective on ISD in general, and ISD methods in particular. Such a perspective, by providing some insight into the past of ISD and ISD methods, helps us understand where we are today, and where we might be moving in the future.

This chapter focuses primarily on methods that follow the systems development life cycle (SDLC). The framework which was introduced in Chapter 2 is modified in Fig. 3.1 to illustrate the issues being discussed in this chapter which is especially concerned with formalised methods and the development context. The chapter is laid out as follows. The nature of early system development and the impetus for the creation of methods leads into a discussion of early techniques and the SDLC. Four major categories of approaches that follow this life cycle model are discussed in the chapter. These include structured (or process-driven) approaches, data-driven approaches, approaches that integrate the process and data perspectives, and object-oriented approaches. Chapter 4 will continue to trace the evolution of methods, focusing on those approaches that are considered somewhat more 'radical' than the methods discussed in this chapter.

Since the purpose of these two chapters is primarily to provide some perspective and insight into the evolution of methods, these chapters do not provide complete

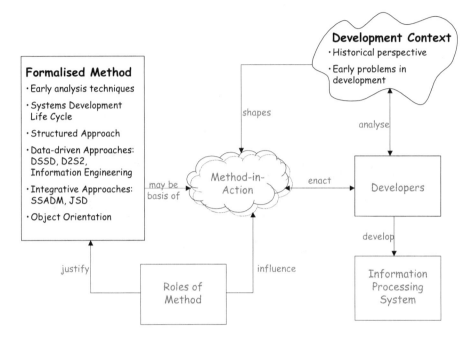

Fig. 3.1   ISD Method Focus in this Chapter

descriptions of the methods discussed. Instead references are frequent, both to books which describe methods directly, and also to research focused on the analysis and evaluation of methods.

3.2   THE EARLY YEARS

In the early years of computing during the 1940s, the computer was primarily used for scientific problem solving. It was needed principally because of its speed of mathematical calculation and was applied in areas such as the calculation of missile trajectories, aerodynamics and seismic data analysis. The users of computers at the time were typically scientific researchers with a strong mathematical or engineering background who developed their own programs to address the particular areas in which they were carrying out research. For example, one of the early computers, ENIAC (Electronic Numerical Integrator and Calculator), which became operational in 1945, was reckoned, by the time it was taken out of service in 1955, to have done more arithmetic than had been done by the whole human race prior to 1945. Given this type of environment, there was little need for direct management control, nor indeed for any method to support development.

During the early 1950s, the use of computers began to spread beyond that of scientific problem solving to address the area of business data processing. These early data processing applications were concerned with the complete and accurate capture of the organisation's business transactions, and with automating routine clerical tasks to make them quicker and more accurate. This trend quickly spread, and by 1960 the business data processing use of computers had overtaken the scientific one. Once underway, the business use of computers accelerated at an extremely rapid rate. The extent of this rapid expansion is evidenced by the fact that in the US, the number of computer installations increased more than twenty-fold between 1960 and 1970 (Lecht, 1977). However, this rapid expansion did not occur without accompanying problems.

3.2.1   Early Problems

The nature of business data processing was very different from the computation-intensive nature of scientific applications. Business applications involve high volumes of input and output, but the input and output peripherals at the time were very slow and inefficient. Also, memory capacity was very limited, and this led to the widespread conviction among developers that good programs were efficient programs, rather than clear, well-documented and easily understood programs. Given these problems, writing programs required much creativity and resourcefulness on the part of the programmer. Indeed, it was recognised that it was a major achievement to get a program to run at all in the early 1960s.

Also, there was no formal training for developers. Programming skills could only be learned through experience. Some programmers were drawn from academic and scientific environments and thus had some prior experience. However, many programmers converted over from a diverse range of departments. Friedman (1989, p. 92) captures the pioneering essence of the time:

> People were drawn from very many areas of the organisation into the DP department, and many regarded it as an 'unlikely' accident that they became involved with computers.

There were no programming standards to help guide these novice programmers. In the absence of standards, the individuality and creativity of developers, coupled with the necessity to write programs to be as concise and efficient as possible, led to the creation of complex programs which were very difficult to understand. Indeed, Dijkstra (1972) described programs written at this time as "conglomerations of idiosyncrasies", in that individual programmers wrote programs in an obscure manner, often taking a measure of satisfaction from the incomprehensibility of their programs. This had the inevitable effect of making the task of program maintenance an extremely difficult one. Allied to the shortage of experienced programmers, programmer turnover was also very high as programmers demonstrated more loyalty to the profession than to the organisations in which they worked. This further exacerbated the difficulty of program maintenance, as the original writers of programs were not available to maintain or even explain any complex or esoteric code.

An essential difference between the scientific programming environment and the emerging business data processing environment was that scientific researchers generally developed their own programs for themselves as the primary users (a phenomenon that has parallels in the more recent open source software phenomenon, which is discussed later in chapters 4 and 10). However, with data processing applications, the system developers were not the actual system users. Thus, the task of determining system requirements involved a potentially problematic communication process. Also, during the 1960s, the computer began to be applied to more complex and less-routine business areas, resulting in the paradoxical situation that as the early programmers improved their skills, there was a corresponding increase in the complexity of the problem areas for which programs had to be written. This further contributed to making the task of specifying system requirements more difficult, and as a consequence multi-person development teams were needed. However, early programmers were not necessarily good communicators. Nor were there any proven and reliable techniques to estimate development time so programmers often bowed to user demands and tried to deliver systems in an unrealistic time schedule and within budget. They were then forced to compromise on system quality if they were to meet these targets.

From the early 1960s, therefore, software problems began to dominate. Indeed, by 1968, at a landmark conference on software engineering, held at Garmisch in Germany, there was an open admission of the extent of these problems, giving rise to the term 'software crisis'. Many conference participants reported the same complaints: systems that exceeded time deadlines and budget targets and that failed to satisfy the business requirements for which they were purportedly developed. As the complexity of the systems which needed to be developed was on the increase, the situation would inevitably be further exacerbated. This led to a pressure to introduce more systematic approaches to development.

3.2.2   Early Techniques for Systems Analysis

As already mentioned, in the early years of business data processing, the focus was very much on programming issues. However, the problems discussed above, which soon became apparent, highlighted the need for a change of focus. Consequently, there emerged a growing appreciation of the systems analysis and design phases of systems development in addition to the program coding phase.

The roots of the early systems analysis techniques lay in industrial engineering practices from several decades earlier. Industrial engineers used process flow charts to depict the flow of materials and the points at which transformations occurred. These were supplemented with forms flow charts which utilised special symbols for files and forms, and were thus more suited to the computer era. These early techniques conveyed too little information and required considerable supplementing with narrative annotation, and thus, they quickly gave way to a 'second generation' of analysis techniques.

The second generation analysis techniques had stronger support for systems analysis, in that they were more complete packages which combined the available analysis techniques (see Colter, 1984; Couger, 1973). An example of a second generation technique was ADS (Accurately Defined Systems, an approach which was used internally at NCR for several years before its publication as a manual in 1968). ADS was a comprehensive organised approach which used a series of interrelated forms to define output, input, computation, historical information and logic definitions. The ADS approach was fundamentally focused on the requirements specification phase of systems development. However, other approaches focused on an earlier phase of systems development, starting from a study of the organisation and its information needs. One of the most significant of these approaches was SOP (Study Organisation Plan) developed by IBM who were strong advocates of the separation of systems analysis and design from program coding. The SOP approach (which was eventually to evolve into the Business Systems Planning (BSP) approach) was concerned with gathering a large and varied set of data to analyse the information needs of the entire organisation.

The third generation analysis techniques had two features which differentiated them from earlier approaches. Firstly, there was much more emphasis on systems for the organisation as a whole than for individual departmental systems. Secondly, the computer itself was to be used to assist the analysis process. An example of an approach from this era was TAG (Time Automated Grid) which was introduced with automated support by IBM in 1966. Using TAG, the developer first recorded output data requirements. From these, one worked backwards to determine the necessary inputs. By examining the elapsed time between inputs and outputs, the need for files was identified, and this was used to create a minimum database for the system.

These approaches were taken a stage further in terms of automation by Donald Teichroew and colleagues at the University of Michigan ISDOS (Information Systems Design and Optimisation System) project. This group produced a problem statement language (PSL) which was designed to represent input and output data elements and the formulae used to compute them. Another component, the problem statement analyser (PSA), analysed the PSL input and produced comprehensive data and function dictionaries, an analysis of data relationships, and, eventually, a machine-readable problem statement which could be used for direct physical system design (Teichroew & Sayani, 1971).

However, these early approaches were not widely used, mainly due to the fact that they were complex and were not well supported—IBM withdrew support for TAG in the late 1960s, for example. However, even though these early approaches were superseded, many of the basic principles inherent in these early approaches have been incorporated. For example, the concern with identifying overall organisational information needs; the concept of starting with the output the system must produce and using this to derive the necessary input; defining an underpinning database; a consideration of process-oriented versus data-oriented issues; graphical representation of system structures; capture of requirements in a formal specification—these have been incorporated to a great extent into later methods such as Information Engineering, Jackson Systems Development and the Structured Approach.

3.2.3   The Systems Development Life-Cycle

The origins of the life-cycle may be traced to general systems theory of the 1930s. However, its introduction into systems development was stimulated by its use in operations research in the 1950s where the reductionist principles of the life-cycle were applied as an approach to problem solving. As computing became more widespread, researchers familiar with the systems approach proposed life-cycle models for system development. An early example of a systems development life cycle was proposed by Canning (1956) and consisted of the following four phases:

- Systems study (includes requirements determination)
- Preliminary design
- Detailed design
- Programming/acquisition/installation

During the 1960s the life-cycle model was modified and elaborated upon. By concentrating on the verification of deliverables from each phase, thus ensuring that each phase be satisfactorily completed before the next one began, the model assumed a 'waterfall' effect, which was how it was presented by Royce (1970) (see Fig. 3.2).

There are a number of fundamental characteristics inherent in the SDLC concept: Firstly, the life-cycle consists of *discrete stages*, each of which has distinct activities and a specific end-product, often documentation, which serves as input to the next stage. Also, there is a *stage-limited commitment* in that at the end of any stage the decision to proceed is only valid until the completion of the next stage, thus giving rise to the 'creeping commitment' phrase which has been used to characterise the approach. At the end of each stage, there is a *signoff of interim end-products*. Thus, stage deliverables are verified and feedback is facilitated to ensure each stage has been

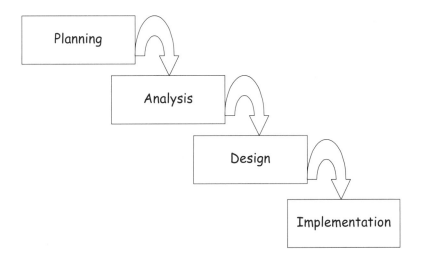

Fig. 3.2   The Waterfall SDLC (adapted from Royce, 1970)

completed satisfactorily. Also, within each stage, there may be several *in-stage reviews* whose purpose is to try identify errors at the earliest possible time.

The life-cycle concept is quite a common approach to problem-solving in many disciplines, and so it is hardly surprising that the life-cycle should have been applied to systems development. However, due to the nature of the software crisis, the SDLC primarily came to be viewed as a prescriptive device to control projects in that it was seen as a checklist to govern when and how different activities should be performed and what resources would be required. However, at a practical level, the rationale behind the SDLC approach had much to recommend it. It ensured a top-down approach, from a broad overall view to technical detail, thereby taking a 'divide and conquer' approach to dealing with complexity. Also, the logical sequence of the steps helped eliminate the problem of premature coding, by enshrining the principle that design should precede coding, and indeed, that requirements analysis should precede design.

The SDLC has evolved as focus and concerns have shifted in the IS field. For example, the early front-end phases of the SDLC expanded to cater for the growing concern with organisational planning issues, while the structured approach, discussed next, caused an expansion in the middle phases of the SDLC. In similar fashion, the latter back-end-phases were expanded to cater for the emphasis on satisfying user needs, and for the development of decision support systems (DSS) where user experience of the system is considered critical to ensure acceptance and use.

3.3   THE STRUCTURED APPROACH

The early work described above had provided little direct benefit for practising developers. However, building on the concepts that emerged from this early work, the primary thrust from the early 1970s was towards the development of coherent methods for systems development. The *structured approach* represented such a development which has gained widespread appeal. It has been suggested to be the most well-known and widely-used development approach in practice (Russo *et al.*, 1995).

The structured approach is based on the waterfall life-cycle. The specification, design, and coding phases inherent in the waterfall model map well to the structured analysis, design, and programming activities of the structured approach. Ironically, the structured approach, which enshrines the basic principle of a top-down approach to systems development with its recommendation that system design should follow a progression from broad outline to technical detail, itself evolved in a bottom-up fashion from structured programming through structured design to structured analysis.

3.3.1   Structured Programming

One of the principal objectives of the Garmisch conference, referred to earlier, was to apply engineering principles, common in other disciplines, to the development of software systems. This emphasis on an engineering approach is evident in early pioneering research in the field (e.g. Dijkstra, 1965; Bohm & Jacopini 1966). The research by Bohm & Jacopini proved that any program could be written using just three basic constructs—sequence, selection and iteration. This research was based on earlier work by Turing, and Von Neumann, and was originally published in 1962, but its eventual publication in English in 1966 was more influential, as it reinforced the ideas of Dijkstra (1965) who suggested that the greatest single problem in programming practice was the undisciplined use of the GOTO statement. This research subsequently led to the structured programming approach which sought to eliminate the esoteric and individualistic approaches to programming at the time. The basic recommendation of the structured programming approach was that programmers should be restricted to using just these three constructs and that unconditional branching be avoided, although some minor refinements were adopted following debate of the issues at the time (cf. Yourdon, 1979).

3.3.2   Structured Design

However, addressing the program coding problem had a limited effect, really only serving to reveal 'pollution' further upstream in the design process. Thus, the focus of interest was enlarged to consider system design. This resulted in the structured design approach which incorporated concepts such as a top-down, functional decomposition approach to program design, and modularisation of program code (Stevens, Myers & Constantine, 1974; Yourdon & Constantine, 1979). Functional decomposition refers to the progressive subdivision of primary functions into sub-functions until some primitive level is reached from which individual program modules are written. This functional decomposition is an example of the 'divide and conquer' approach which allows one to break a complex task into more manageable sub-tasks, and it has been the basis of mathematical problem-solving for centuries. Also, by taking a modular approach, several developers can work fairly independently, thus allowing teams of developers to work in parallel on development projects.

To this end, principles such as *information hiding*—the idea that each module should hide exactly one design decision and reveal as little as possible about its inner workings or the data it uses (Parnas, 1972)—came to be a central tenet of structured design. Two other related topics are *cohesion* and *coupling* which are both important to ensure a correct approach to modularisation. These concepts are explained in some detail in DeMarco (1978). Cohesion refers to the extent to which an individual module is self-contained and performs a single well-defined function. Coupling, on the other hand, refers to the degree of interdependence of modules, that is the extent to which changes to any particular module affect other modules. A high degree of module cohesiveness is desirable, as is a low degree of module coupling. Other techniques which form part of structured design are *structure charts*—a graphical representation of the system structure, *mini-specifications*—a 'half-way house' between English and a programming language which allow a terse and unambiguous representation of module logic using just the permissible structured programming constructs, and *transform analysis* and *transaction analysis*—different strategies which can be used to decompose functions. These techniques are fully described in DeMarco (1978).

3.3.3 Structured Analysis

Again, a deficiency became apparent with the structured design approach in that it was of little use to have well-designed and well-structured systems if they were not able to solve the basic problem they set out to address. So, the focus shifted to consideration of analysis of the problem domain giving rise to the structured analysis approach. The principal tools and techniques of structured analysis are Data Flow Diagrams (DFDs), Entity Relationship Diagrams (ERDs) and the Data Dictionary. Again, these are thoroughly documented in DeMarco (1978).

Two principal development methods for structured analysis have emerged. One is based around the work of Yourdon and colleagues, and is well-documented (DeMarco, 1978; Gane & Sarson, 1977; Yourdon & Constantine, 1979). This ecumenical approach has achieved widespread adoption as the most popular development method in North America and Europe (Yourdon, 1991). The other structured analysis approach arose from the Structured Analysis and Design Technique (SADT) (Ross & Brackett, 1976). This method was initially marketed in a different way to the Yourdon flavour as it was only available under a very expensive licence from a company called SofTech, and it has been used extensively by the US airforce. Hence, the SADT flavour of structured analysis achieved a narrower but deeper penetration than the Yourdon version.

3.3.4   Impact of the Structured Approach

The structured approach was one of the first panaceas, or 'silver bullets' to use Brooks' (1987) term, in the software industry. Indeed, it was labelled as the 'universal elixir' by Glass (1977), and, as mentioned earlier, is suggested to be the most popular and widely-used methodology in North America and Europe. By coupling technical elements with more management-oriented elements, such as walk-throughs, team reviews, phase deliverables and signoffs, the structured approach represented a development method which could be sold in the form of training courses, seminars or books.

One might reasonably expect that such a popular method would have been rigorously derived. Firstly through an independent peer review process, whereby experts in the area, who have no vested interest in the method, would examine it for shortcomings. Secondly, by obtaining empirical evidence of usability through the successful application of the method in a non-trivial development situation. However, neither of these processes appear to have been actually followed for the structured approach. Ward, who was one of the leading figures in the development of the structured approach, has documented its evolution (Ward, 1991, 1992a, 1992b). He refers to the original founders of the structured approach as the "Boston system development Mafia" given that the majority were former students at MIT. He describes how the landmark books (DeMarco, 1978; Gane & Sarson, 1977) documenting the approach were rushed into print in a few months (Ward, 1992a). Indeed, Constantine admits that the early "investigations ... were no more than noon hour critiques" (Yourdon & Constantine, 1977). The authors relied on intuition rather than real-world experience that the techniques would work. However, a number of criticisms and weaknesses have been identified.

Firstly, the representational shift required to move from the analysis stage to the design stage is a major weakness in the structured approach. The creation of hierarchical structure charts from data flow diagrams is poorly defined, thus causing the design to be loosely coupled to the results of the analysis (Colter, 1982). Coad & Yourdon (1991) label this shift as a "grand canyon" due to its fundamental discontinuity. DeMarco, who had to solve this problem of making the transition from data flow modelling of analysis to structure chart modelling of design, proposed a four-step sequence of modelling the current physical system, the current logical system, the new logical system and the new physical system. This last step was used to derive structure charts. However, trying to achieve this four-step sequence saw many practitioners floundering in the "current physical tarpit". De Marco has since himself admitted that the four-step sequence was a mistake (Ward, 1992a). Indeed, McMenamin & Palmer (1984) modified the approach to eliminate the modelling of the current physical system in proposing their Essential Systems Analysis method. Henson & Hughes (1991) have also criticised the logical/physical separation of the structured approach pointing out that logical solutions could be proposed which could turn out to be physically impossible to implement.

Friedman (1989) reported that interviews with practitioners revealed that many of the concepts underpinning the structured approach were being used implicitly by practitioners anyway. However, an empirical survey of practitioners (Sumner & Sitek, 1986) found that while practitioners generally acknowledged the benefits of the structured approach, quite often, they did not actually use the structured approach in practice. Two of the main obstacles to use cited by respondents in the Sumner & Sitek study were the fact that the method was too time-consuming to use, and also its lack of acceptance, especially by end-users (ironically, the participation of end-users is suggested to be enhanced by the structured approach).

Bergland (1981) also addressed this issue. He suggested that some of the structured techniques, such as programmer teams, design and code reviews and walk-throughs, were readily applied, while other more fundamental concepts, including the necessity of having well-structured programs, were not so readily implemented. Thus, the structured approach may not in practice be implemented in its entirety as a development method, but individual concepts and techniques are probably widely used.

The structured approach represents one of the 'hard' development methods and does not address softer issues. For example, Bansler and Bodker (1993, p. 171) criticised it due to its disregarding of the "problems posed by differing *interests* and *power*", and its failure to recognise the need for negotiating and establishing consensus among users about the purpose of the new system.

In a review of the structured approach, another of its pioneering figures, Gane (1991), suggested that the structured approach has been successful because its concepts are now so well assimilated that it appears to be disappearing. Gane identified three major principles as the legacy of the structured approach. Firstly, its emphasis on the importance of making programs maintainable, which results from the increased clarity of having well-structured programs that only use the standard constructs (see structured programming section above). Secondly, its facilitation of the changeability of programs due to adherence to information hiding, cohesion and coupling guidelines (see structured design section above). The third part of the legacy is the improved visibility of the system design which results from the use of graphical models for representing system structure. This lack of visibility inherent in software systems has been identified by Brooks (1987) as one of the essential difficulties in the software field.

It is worth noting that Yourdon, the principal originator of the structured approach, has twice (Yourdon, 1988, 1991) stated that the structured approach is "irrelevant" and "obsolete" given the modern development environment. The structured approach is essentially a process-oriented one, and thus it failed, in its initial conceptions at any rate, to cater for the data-oriented dimension. Data-driven approaches to systems development are discussed next.

3.4   DATA DRIVEN APPROACHES

Most early applications of computerisation involved the automation of manual processes and procedures, and thus, a functional, process-oriented perspective dominated early methods. As Palmer (1991) explained it: "computers were able to perform functions long before they could implement databases", so this perspective was a natural one. The structured approach, having the central concepts and techniques of functional decomposition, data flow diagrams, structure charts and mini-specifications, was essentially a process-driven one, although various techniques were incorporated to redress the balance in favour of data-oriented and event-oriented perspectives.

Process-oriented approaches suffer from a fundamental problem in that processes are quite volatile and prone to change. By contrast, the data structures that comprise a system are generally far less volatile. Consequently, a data-driven approach should represent a more stable underpinning for systems development, and thus a number of development methods emerged which adopted a data-driven perspective (Chen, 1976; Jackson, 1975, 1983; Martin & Finkelstein, 1981; Orr, 1977; Warnier, 1976). It seems that the process-driven approach was more popular in the US, while the data-driven approach was more popular in Europe (Beynon-Davies, 1989).

Just as magnetic tape storage had been an important facilitator to the emergence of data processing in the late 1950s with its enabling of file storage, the proliferation of disk storage and the emergence of database management systems played an important enabling role in the rise to prominence of data-driven approaches. Also, much research had been conducted in the area of data analysis and modelling (e.g. Chen, 1976).

3.4.1   Data Structured Systems Development (DSSD)

Among the first researchers to propose a data-driven approach to systems development were Warnier (1976) and Orr (1977). Orr's *data-structured systems development*

(DSSD) method was based on a realisation from practical experience that successful solutions were often those in which the program structure mirrored that of the data. DSSD began as a program-design method, focused on working backwards from data outputs through to ideal inputs, but subsequently evolved into a full systems development method dealing with database design, requirements definition, and systems planning and architecture (Orr, 1989). As well as finding parallels in the work of Warnier, Orr has admitted to having been influenced by Jackson (1975) who was also pursuing a data-driven design approach.

3.4.2   Development of Data Sharing Systems (D2S2)

Another significant development method with a primarily data-driven focus emerged in the UK in the D2S2 (Development of Data Sharing Systems) method from the CACI organisation who are recognised to have been a "powerhouse of knowledge" and a very influential source for some of the leading authorities on development methods (Holloway, 1989). The D2S2 method was documented in detail by Palmer & Rock Evans (1981) and has been applied on many projects in Europe since 1975 (Holloway, 1989). It has also evolved to incorporate the other approaches to system development, and it was an important influence in the emergence of Information Engineering, which is discussed next.

3.4.3   Information Engineering

The origins of Information Engineering are not universally agreed upon. However, the work of Martin & Finkelstein (1981) and Martin (1982) is generally cited, as is the influence of the CACI method, D2S2. Among the basic premises of Information Engineering are the following: data structures are quite stable and lie at the centre of modern data processing; communication among developers and users is greatly facilitated by the use of graphical representations; and an overall organisational strategic orientation is necessary in systems development. Martin (1984) has argued that the software engineering and structured approaches were neither comprehensive nor sophisticated enough to solve the problems of systems development, and were biased towards a process-driven perspective. A fundamental tenet of Information Engineering is that data is an important organisational resource and should be managed accordingly. Martin (1984) also suggested that contemporary approaches to systems development did not have an overall enterprise orientation, but were primarily concerned with individual applications. One of the main recommendations of the Information Engineering method is that organisations create an overall enterprise model which can form the basis for all systems development. This allows a co-ordinated approach and eliminates some of the data redundancy problems inherent in systems developed around functional processes. Also, an explicit

Analysis Phase
> Project Scope Stage
> Strategic Modelling Stage
>> Strategic modelling
>> Strategic objectives modelling
>> Strategic refinement
> Tactical Modelling Stage
>> Tactical modelling
>> Tactical objectives modelling
>> Tactical refinement
> Operations Modelling Stage
>> Current systems modelling

Design Phase
> Strategic Design Stage
> Tactical and Operations Design Stage

Generation Phase
> Implementation Strategies Stage
> Systems Generation Stage

Table 3.1   Phases of Information Engineering (from Finkelstein, 1989)

objective of Information Engineering is to automate as much of the development process as possible (Finkelstein, 1989).

The Information Engineering method has been evolving in different streams due to the many companies that have been set up by James Martin based on the method. It is a very comprehensive method which was documented initially in Martin & Finkelstein (1981), and later in Martin (1989) and Finkelstein (1989). In the latter, the Information Engineering method is presented as having a strategic planning focus encompassing three broad phases: analysis, design and generation, with each of these phases further subdivided into a number of stages (see Table 3.1).

3.5   INTEGRATIVE APPROACHES: PROCESS-DRIVEN AND DATA-DRIVEN

In addition to data and process perspectives, a *behaviour* or *state* perspective has also been recognised as an important dimension for systems development. As Yourdon (1988) described it:

> Since most systems are complex in three different dimensions—functions, data, timing and control—it is useful to have three different types of models, Data Flow Diagrams,

Entity Relationship Diagrams, and State Transition Diagrams, each of which illustrates a single perspective of the system.

The approaches discussed up to now were primarily focused, in their initial conceptions at any rate, on just one of these perspectives. However, a number of methods began with a more pluralist outlook, integrating these perspectives from the outset. Examples of such integrative approaches include Structured Systems Analysis and Design Method (SSADM) and Jackson System Development (JSD).

3.5.1   Structured Systems Analysis and Design Method

SSADM had its foundations in the MODUS development method which was formulated by BIS Applied Systems in 1965. In 1977, two BIS consultants, Learmonth and Burchett set up their own company LBMS (Learmonth Burchett Management Systems). Then, in 1980, the UK government body, the Central Computer and Telecommunications Agency (CCTA) tendered for the provision of a comprehensive systems development method. Almost fifty products from the US, UK and Europe were evaluated and LBMS won the contract, resulting in the development of the SSADM method which has been mandatory on UK government projects since 1983.

Despite its title, SSADM is not generally recognised as being part of the structured approach. The method has its origins in a primarily data-driven approach, but it emerged as a truly integrative method, incorporating structured programming constructs and event-modelling techniques which are similar to those in Jackson Structured Programming and Jackson System Design (Jackson, 1983), and also the structured analysis ideas of Gane & Sarson (1977).

In 1987, the CCTA launched a major drive to promote the method and the National Computing Centre (NCC) were invited to help with marketing and provide documentation and training. The method has proven immensely popular in the UK—indeed, Beynon-Davies (1989) suggested, at that time, that information systems development in the UK had "become almost exclusively associated with … SSADM". The SSADM method was estimated to be used on projects totalling billions of pounds each year in the UK alone (Downs *et al.*, 1992), and a large number of organisations now supply consultancy, training, and CASE tools supporting the SSADM method. SSADM expects the use of computer tools, and products such as AutoMate, DataMate, LEAP, PromptII, Select SSADM and Quickbuild have been designed to work with SSADM. Other governments which have also adopted SSADM as the required development method include Hong Kong, Ireland, Israel and Malta.

The method is very comprehensive and is generally used on medium to large projects although some 'cut-down' versions have been proposed which are more suited to rapid development (see Chapter 4) or smaller projects—Micro-SSADM (Avison & Fitzgerald, 1995) and "Rapid SSADM" (Hargrave, 1995), for example. It has evolved considerably over the years with a breakdown of the formal structures of earlier versions and an emphasis that the method specifies *guidelines*, not *rigid rules*, for software development. This is intended to allow for the contingencies of different development situations, and the method explicitly identifies particular stages at which the process may be customised to suit the situation at hand. The method is very comprehensive, and comprises a hierarchy of modules, stages, steps and tasks, which serve to divide the development process into a number of phases, each of which use standard documents and produce deliverables which help review progress and form a basis for subsequent phases (see Table 3.2).

3.5.2   Jackson System Development

The Jackson System Development (JSD) method has grown out of the Jackson Structured Programming (JSP) program design method which had a significant effect on programming practice, and which came to be widely-used. The JSP method has been applied in several application areas and is well documented (cf. Jackson, 1975; Ingevaldsson, 1979; King & Pardoe, 1985; Sanden, 1985; Storer, 1987). In formulating JSP, Jackson identified weaknesses in the structured programming concept of top-down functional decomposition, in that it was an abstract concept which relied very much on intuition and creativity on the part of the programmer. As Storer (1987, p. 12) described it:

> Top-down design requires the designer to subdivide one abstract unknown quantity into increasingly detailed and known quantities, but if the original quantity is an unknown, on what basis is that subdivision to take place? The answer is intuition, experience and trial and error.

In contrast, JSP sought to eliminate the need for invention or insight on the part of the programmer. Jackson identified the following characteristics of JSP: It is non-inspirational and teachable, thus ensuring that different programmers will produce similar programs given a particular development situation. The method is also practical and easy to understand, thus making it quite accessible to the average programmer. Jackson further suggested that the method is based on reasoned and rational principles which can be validated.

A basic premise of JSP is that the relationships of the real world should be reflected in the computer model. Therefore, JSP does not begin with abstract functions which are then progressively refined; rather it is concerned with modelling the real-world problem situation. JSP also departed from the structured approach discussed earlier, in that it adopted a data-driven perspective. Jackson adapted the Bohm & Jacopini (1966) result which proved that programs could be written using just three basic constructs to show that all data structures could also be represented using just

Module 1: Feasibility Study (FS)
    Stage 0: Feasibility
    Steps:
      010   Prepare for Feasibility Study
      020   Define the Problem
      030   Select Feasibility Option
      040   Assemble Feasibility Report

Module 2: Requirements Analysis (RA)
    Stage 1: Investigation of Current Environment
    Steps:
      110   Establish Analysis Framework
      120   Investigate and Define Requirements
      130   Investigate Current Processing
      140   Investigate Current Data
      150   Derive Logical View of Current Services
      160   Assemble Investigation Results
    Stage 2: Business System Options
    Steps:
      210   Define Business System Options
      220   Select Business System Option

Module 3: Requirements Specification (RS)
    Stage 3: Definition of Requirements
    Steps:
      310   Define Required System Processing
      320   Develop Required Data Model
      330   Derive System Functions
      340   Enhance Required Data Model
      350   Develop Specification Prototypes
      360   Develop Processing Specification
      370   Confirm System Objectives
      380   Assemble Requirements Specification

Module 4: Logical System Specification (LS)
    Stage 4: Technical System Options
    Steps:
      410   Define Technical System Options
      420   Select Technical System Options
    Stage 5: Logical Design
    Steps:
      510   Define User Dialogues
      520   Define Update Processes
      530   Define Enquiry Processes
      540   Assemble Logical Design

Module 5: Physical Design (PS)
    Stage 6: Physical Design
    Steps:
      610   Prepare for Physical Design
      620   Create Physical Data Design
      630   Create Function Component Implementation Map
      640   Optimise Physical Data Design
      650   Complete Function Specification
      660   Consolidate Process Data Interface
      670   Assemble Physical Design

Table 3.2   Steps of SSADM Method (from Downs *et al.*, 1992)

these constructs. The JSP method, rather than following a process of decomposition, advocates a process of composition in which program structures are composed from data structures.

Jackson System Design is an outgrowth of JSP. The JSD method adopts a primarily data-driven perspective, but it also recognises the central importance of the time dimension, inherent in real world applications (Jackson, 1983). JSD begins by modelling the real world components of the problem situation, and synthesising these into a system specification. Explicit consideration of systems functions and processes are deferred until later steps in the method. JSD is fully documented in Jackson (1983) and also well described in Cameron (1986). The JSD method encompasses three main phases, the Model phase, the Network phase, and the Implementation phase. The Model phase is the initial one, and is concerned with modelling the relevant actions and entities and their attributes, thus defining the scope of the system. The Network phase builds a specification from the model which comprises largely disconnected sequential processes. New processes are added and existing processes elaborated on. Finally, the Implementation phase is concerned with two main issues: running the processes that comprise the specification, and storing the data that they contain. These three broad phases comprise the following steps, illustrated in Table 3.3:

Entity/Action Step

A definition of the entities and actions of interest in the problem environment.

Entity Structure Step

Entities are determined in terms of actions ordered in time. This entity life-history information is modelled in structure diagrams.

Initial Model Step

This step serves to connect the definitions from earlier steps to the real world. Operations or processes are allocated to the structure diagrams.

Function Step

The first three steps serve as the basis on which system functions are specified. At this stage, the functions which produce outputs are specified and any additional processes incorporated.

System Timing Step

In this step, timing requirements are determined. These may not be obvious in the function model, and these details can constrain implementation choices later.

Implementation Step

The hardware and software platforms are determined, databases are defined, and scheduling issues resolved, thus helping to ensure system efficiency.

Table 3.3   Steps in JSD (from Jackson 1983)

3.5.3   Summary of Process-Driven and Data-Driven Perspectives

The process-driven and data-driven development approaches discussed above have been presented as though they adhered strictly to just one of these perspectives. However, this characterisation is perhaps a little unfair, since as each approach evolved, it adopted concepts and techniques to redress the balance somewhat in favour of the other perspectives. For example, the structured approach was initially very much process-driven (Yourdon & Constantine, 1977). Although the Gane & Sarson (1977) and the DeMarco (1978) versions incorporated data modelling to some extent, it was still subordinate to the process view. According to Ward's (1992b) account of the evolution of the structured approach, by the early 1980s, the data perspective began to be a serious consideration with the incorporation of Flavin's (1981) information modelling concepts. Ward reports that many systems development practitioners were slow to accept the data perspective, and he also admits that many of the pioneering figures of the structured approach were not satisfied with the prominence of the data perspective. Yourdon (1991, p. 42) has since admitted that this was mainly due to commercial interests:

> *In 1975 Michael Jackson's JSP methodology was greeted with some curiosity and mild interest by the technical staff at Yourdon inc., but the marketing staff saw it as a distinct threat and attacked it with the fervor of white blood cells going after a virus. 4GLs, prototyping, data modelling, and all manner of alternative approaches to systems development were also threats.*

In the 1980s, the behaviour or state perspective of systems development was incorporated into the structured approach when it became apparent that the structured approach was better suited to business data processing systems development rather than real-time systems development. This development was influenced by the work of McMenamin & Palmer (1984) who had proposed event-response modelling as an alternative to functional decomposition as a basis for system design. This led to the incorporation of the *state transition diagram* (STD) into the structured approach. The real-time extensions to the structured approach are documented in the work of Ward & Mellor (1985) and Hatley & Pirbhai (1988).

The structured approach was not the only method to incorporate different perspectives as it evolved. Holloway (1989) reports that the CACI method, D2S2, described above, was primarily data-oriented until 1977, when functional decomposition and data flow diagrams were introduced to cater for the process dimension. Later, *entity life-cycles* were incorporated to allow for a behaviour or state perspective, thus making the method more applicable to all types of systems development situations, rather than just those that are primarily database applications. Likewise, Orr (1989) describes how extensions were incorporated into the DSSD method to cope with the state dimension for real-time systems, and *assembly line diagrams* were introduced to deal with process aspects.

3.6   OBJECT-ORIENTED APPROACHES

Although object-oriented approaches are often considered to be 'modern', the origins of object-orientation (OO) can be traced directly to the Simula programming language in use in Norway from 1967, and also before this, OO principles such as encapsulation were used in the design of the Minuteman missile in the late 1950s (Dyke & Kunz, 1989). This section begins by identifying the basic principles of the OO approach and some of its suggested advantages. Following this, object-oriented methods (OOMs)[1] are discussed.

3.6.1   Principles of Object Orientation

As discussed above, most of the traditional approaches to systems development tended to adopt either a process-driven (functional) or a data-driven perspective. However, the OO approach represents a paradigm shift in that what has been termed the artificial distinction between data and process is not made (Coad & Yourdon, 1991). Rather, the attributes of the data structure and the operations (or methods) that it may legitimately perform are encapsulated in a single entity, termed an object. A number of fundamental concepts arise in the context of OO. These include object, encapsulation, classes and inheritance, messaging and polymorphism. These concepts are defined briefly here.

As with many areas in the IS field, there are many divergent views on what object-orientation means. However, there is fairly general agreement on the definition of the term *object*. Martin & Odell (1992) provide the following definition:

> An object is any thing, real or abstract, about which we store data and those methods that manipulate the data.

The basic principle of binding data and methods into an object is referred to as *encapsulation*. Rather than designing data structures that will allow data to be available to all functions in the organisations, as seen in data-driven approaches, the goal when following an object-oriented approach is to closely link data to its related operations within an object, with minimal interfaces with other objects (Mathiassen *et al.*, 2000). This is similar to the concept of information hiding

---

[1] The dilemma of method v. methodology is even more problematic in the OO area, as method here has a particular meaning as a service or function which an object can perform.

(Parnas, 1972). Thus, the internal structure of an object is hidden from other objects, and can only be accessed by the methods of the object itself. This provides certain advantages in terms of facilitating reusability and maintenance. These advantages are discussed in a subsequent section.

Objects tend to cluster into categories that have similar characteristics and operations. This gives rise to higher level category, that of similar sets of objects. This is defined as a *class* (Pressman, 1987). The value of the class concept arises from its facilitation of *inheritance*. The latter allows objects or sub-classes of a parent class (or super-class) to inherit the common data and methods of the parent class. Thus, when specifying an object, it is only necessary to consider the differences between the object and its parent class, as the common data and methods can be inherited automatically. Inheritance hierarchies are also referred to as generalisation-specialisation structures (Coad & Yourdon, 1991; Thomann, 1994).

Since data and methods are encapsulated within objects, the need for communication between objects arises. This is accomplished through the use of *messaging* whereby a message is passed to an object requesting that a particular method be performed. However, coupling is low as the message does not need to know how the actual operation will be performed. This phenomenon is labelled *polymorphism*, that is, a generic message can be sent to several different objects, without needing to specify any implementation details. Indeed, the objects can all respond differently to the same message. Thus, polymorphism allows change to be accommodated more transparently.

3.6.2   Advantages of Object Orientation

Researchers have identified several advantages which may be realised through application of the OO approach. These advantages arise from its suggested natural applicability to the real-world, its power as a modelling technique, and its facilitation of reuse. Each of these have further related benefits which are discussed below.

As mentioned already, the OO approach does not make the artificial distinction between data and process, thus affording a more natural modelling of real-world problem domains (cf. Mathiassen *et al.*, 2000). In fact, Due (1992) has suggested that because of the modelling power of OO, about 10 to 25 basic object models may be enough to represent any business enterprise. The improved modelling capability of OO has several related benefits. For example, communication between developers and users is improved since a more natural model of the business domain is realised. This can help to eliminate costly requirements specification errors (cf. Boehm, 1981). The facilitation of communication between developers and users is all the more desirable given the increasing complexity of systems that are currently being developed. In fact, the improved interaction between developers and users means that more challenging problem domains can be tackled (Coad, 1993).

Additionally, the natural richness of OO modelling eliminates the need to use separate representation modes for analysis and design—entity relationship models and program structure charts, for example. With the OO approach, a single representation is used throughout the life-cycle, with terms and concepts identified during analysis persisting right through to appear in the eventual program code.

The assembly of a class library of fully-tested objects which can be modified precisely through inheritance greatly facilitates reuse, which, while not an advantage unique to OO, is nevertheless greatly facilitated when following the OO approach. This reuse can improve productivity as developers are not required to reinvent the wheel in every development situation.

Also, since the objects being reused may be drawn from a fully-tested class library, and since the increased communication between developers and users can reduce requirements errors, there should be less need for maintenance subsequently. Additionally, given the low coupling between objects and high cohesion achieved through encapsulation and polymorphism, changes are much more localised and easy to deal with, not causing ripple-on effects throughout the system.

3.6.3   Object-Oriented Methods

More than 30 object-oriented methods (OOMs) have been published to date, although these vary from academic exercises to those which have been applied by experienced developers in real-life systems development. In addition to these new OOMs, there has been considerable interest in converting existing methods to OO, specifically, the structured approach (Ward, 1989), Multiview (cf. Jayaratna, 1993) and NIAM (Creasy & Hesse, 1994).

The issue of whether OO represents a completely new paradigm (Thomann, 1994) or an outgrowth of the structured approach (Ward, 1989) has also been of source of conflict. A number of researchers have addressed this issue, proposing various classifications of OOMs (Berard, 1995; Dock, 1992; Monarchi & Puhr, 1992). Table 3.4 has been constructed to summarise this research, and its components are discussed below. Although each OO method is not discussed in detail here, references are included in Table 3.4.

Berard (1995) draws on Yourdon to make a distinction between evolutionary and revolutionary OOMs. He characterises evolutionary approaches as similar to traditional ones, using graphical techniques such as DFDs, treating objects as if they were data, i.e. viewing them as static and modelling them as compatible with relational data stores. Evolutionary approaches also propose separate functional and data models. Berard classifies Embley-Kurtz, FUSION, Martin & Odell, OMT, and Shlaer-Mellor as evolutionary OOMs.

Revolutionary approaches, in Berard's view, place heavy emphasis on OO concepts—inheritance and polymorphism, for example. They draw on OO program-

Method	Evolutionary/ revolutionary	Completeness	Robust?	Combinative/ Adaptive/ Pure OO
Bailin (1989)				Adaptive
BOOM (Berard, 1993)	Revolutionary			
Coad-Yourdon OOA/OOD (Coad & Yourdon, 1991)		b, d−−		Combinative
Embley-Kurtz (Embley et al., 1992)	Evolutionary			Combinative
FUSION (Coleman et al.,1994)	Evolutionary	b, d−−		
MOSES (Henderson-Sellers & Edwards, 1994)				Adaptive
Objectory/OOSE (Jacobson et al., 1992)		b, d	Yes	Pure OO
OMT (Rumbaugh et al., 1991)	Evolutionary	b, d++	Yes	Combinative
Ptech (Martin & Odell, 1992)	Evolutionary			Combinative
Rational Booch (Booch 1994)	Revolutionary	b, d++	Yes	Pure OO
RDD (Wirfs-Brock et al., 1990)	Revolutionary	b−−, d		Pure OO
Shlaer-Mellor (Shlaer & Mellor, 1991)	Evolutionary	b, d	Yes	Combinative

b = breadth, b++ = good breadth, b−− = poor depth, d = depth, d++ = good depth, d−− = poor depth

Table 3.4 Summary of Object-Oriented Methods

ming languages, emphasise the active nature of objects, and show a clear separation between classes and instances, with functionality included within classes. Examples of revolutionary OOMs are BOOM, Booch and RDD.

Berard's classification is similar to that of another widely-cited typology of OOMs, that of Monarchi & Puhr (1992). The latter classify OOMs as combinative, adaptive, and pure OO approaches. Combinative approaches use OO techniques along with traditional function-oriented and state-oriented techniques together with a way of integrating these models. OOMs such as Coad-Yourdon, Embley-Kurtz, OMT, Ptech, and Shlaer-Mellor may be classified as combinative. Adaptive approaches use traditional techniques in a new (OO) way or extend existing techniques to include OO. Methods that fall into this category include Bailin and MOSES, according to Monarchi and Puhr. Pure OO approaches use new OO techniques to model object structure, functionality and behaviour. This category includes OOMs such as RDD, Booch, and Objectory/OOSE.

Berard (1995) also classifies OOMs according to completeness and robustness. Completeness has two dimensions, breadth (how much of the life-cycle is covered and which activities are addressed) and depth (to what level of detail each activity is covered). Robustness has a number of dimensions, including the length of time the method has been in use, the number of projects it has been used on, literature references and general completeness. OOMs with good breadth but little depth include FUSION and Coad-Yourdon. OOMs with more depth than breadth include Booch, OMT, and RDD. OOMs which have both include Objectory/OOSE and Shlaer-Mellor. In terms of robustness, Booch, OMT, Shlaer-Mellor and Objectory/OOSE are classified as robust (see Table 3.4).

A recent entrant to the OOM field, called OOA&D (Object-Oriented Analysis and Design), broadens the focus of the OOM to address the context of the system (Mathiassen et al., 2000). This analysis and design method encompasses four main activities: problem-domain analysis, application-domain analysis, architectural design, and component design. Programming and quality assurance activities would complete the life cycle. The authors of the method propose alternative ways to implement the method, including a traditional top-down approach and an incremental approach. Interestingly, an important tenet of the method is to tailor the method to specific projects.

3.6.4   Summary of Object-Oriented Approaches

As already mentioned, the OO approach is not new, having antecedents in projects almost forty years ago. Also, as illustrated above, it may be regarded in many respects as an evolutionary outgrowth of more traditional approaches. The surge in interest in the topic has tended to equate "object orientation with every boy-scout virtue known to man" (Yourdon, 1991). The suggested advantages of OO, as reviewed briefly above, are certainly significant. However, much of the research and practice in the OO area to date has been in fringe areas outside the commercial mainstream of business information processing. For example, the areas of graphics, user interface design, simulation, and chip design have all benefited greatly from the OO approach. Part of the explanation for the concentration on these areas lies in the fact that OO applications have been the preserve of computer scientists and academics who have used it in areas of familiarity and interest to themselves. These researchers are typically unfamiliar with business problem domains and have not applied OO to these areas. OO is now being applied in commercial and mainstream business applications. However, researchers have argued that OO methods need to evolve further before they can cater for business situations, as most of the applications of OO in the past have been in problem domains where object persistence, a prerequisite for business information systems, is not relevant (Thomann, 1994). That is, in a system to support the functioning of some laboratory equipment such as an oscilloscope, or in an elevator control system, once the system is functioning, all the necessary information can be readily determined online in real-time. These states can be reconstituted, and generally, very little information needs to be retained in a persistent form after the system shuts down. However, in a business context where customers or invoices may be modelled as objects, then the persistent retention of this information is critical, and needs to be faithfully reproducible for subsequent sessions following system shutdown. Thus, object persistence is critical in business applications.

The take-up of OO on real projects in practice is not all that clear-cut. Firesmith (1992), for example, reported the findings of a study of 23 projects using an OO programming language, *none* of which were taking full advantage of OO principles. Other studies of method use have shown only a very small number of organisations using an OOM as a primary development method (Russo & Wynekoop, 2000). Firesmith offers a number of practical guidelines to help introduce OO in organisations. These guidelines indicate that it takes several projects before benefits are evident, and managerial issues are as important as technical issues.

An approach to development that is very much premised on OO principles is that of eXtreme Programming (cf. Beck, 2000). While it is not an approach that consciously classifies itself as OO in the same manner as the methods described above, the approach more or less takes for granted that development will take place in an OO environment with classes, superclasses, and encapsulated methods in the OO sense of the word. eXtreme Programming (XP) will be discussed in more detail in Chapter 4.

3.7 CHAPTER SUMMARY

ISD methods have evolved in response to a need for structure, formalisation, and documentation in the system development process. Early techniques were imported from industrial engineering and were primarily used to document process flows. Gradually techniques were added to address not only the design of programs but also to support analysis and requirements specification. Paralleling the creation of techniques to support the development process was the recognition that the process itself could be viewed in more systematic terms. In particular, the principles of the systems development life cycle (SDLC) were applied to the ISD process. There are many variations of the SDLC, but generally it breaks the development process into some number of discrete phases, typically beginning with planning or requirements determination and ending with the implementation of the operational system. Hundreds, possibly even thousands, of methods have been based on the SDLC. The methods discussed in this chapter have been grouped together into those that follow the structured or process-driven approach, those that are data-oriented, those that integrate the process and data perspectives, and those that follow the object-oriented approach. The following chapter will describe approaches and corresponding methods that do not have the life cycle as their underlying structure.

3.8   DISCUSSION QUESTIONS

1.   Given the history of its emergence, problems in ISD were perhaps inevitable. Identify and discuss some of the historical factors that have led to these problems.

2.   The evolution of ISD methods reveals a progression from a concern with programming issues, through design issues to analysis issues. This happened with both the structured approach and object orientation. Why do you think this bottom-up progression from narrow to broad occurs so often with IS phenomena? Is the situation similar in other disciplines?

3.   Some suggest that the solution to the problems of ISD lie in the use of more formal, mathematically-based methods for requirements specification and program design. Do you think these methods are suited to ISD in general?

4.   More experienced (and invariably often older) ISD practitioners and academics have been trained in the traditional approach which separates data and processes. As a result, they do not cope naturally with object orientation which integrates data and processes. Less experienced (and invariably often younger) ISD practitioners and academics have been trained in object orientation from the outset and use the concept naturally. What kind of problems in teaching and practice might this lead to?

The 'Radical' Approaches – The Evolution Continues

4.1   INTRODUCTION

This chapter continues the historical overview of ISD and ISD methods. Again, the framework which was introduced in Chapter 2 is refined in Fig. 4.1 to illustrate the particular issues being discussed in this chapter. The methods discussed in this chapter are those that do not necessarily follow the traditional system development life cycle (SDLC). Among the approaches considered are Rapid Application Development (RAD) and eXtreme Programming (XP). In addition to following a somewhat different pattern of activities, the overall focus of some of these methods are quite different. In several of these methods, there is less of an emphasis on technology, and more emphasis on the 'soft' human and organisational elements of system development, and the dynamic nature of the development process. The chapter also discusses Software Process Improvement and the Capability Maturity Model. Whereas this is not a method in itself, it does impact the way that organisations develop systems. The two final sections of the chapter deal with ERP systems and open source software respectively. ERP systems represent perhaps the ultimate in package software development which has become a significant factor in ISD today. While the open source software (OSS) phenomenon is quite a recent one (cf. Feller and Fitzgerald, 2002), it seems to have major implications for the future of IS development. These issues are discussed again in Chapter 10.

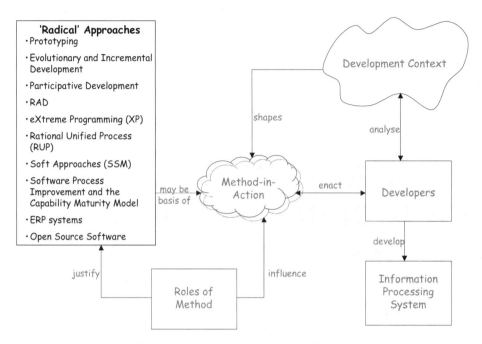

Fig. 4.1 Focus Adopted in this Chapter

4.2 THE PROTOTYPING APPROACH

As mentioned in the previous chapter, most development methods follow some variation of the systems development life cycle. However, two major systems development problems are the length of time for systems development from initial conception to eventual delivery—which can be several years (Harel & McLean, 1985)—and the fact that systems are often delivered which fail to solve the problems for which they were originally developed, largely because of fundamental errors in the specification of system requirements in the first place. Researchers have argued that these problems are due to the nature of the SDLC itself (Gladden, 1982; Glass, 1991; McCracken & Jackson, 1981) and these issues are considered here.

Different estimates have been made as to completion times for systems development. For example, Flaatten *et al.* (1989) estimated development time to be about 18 months on average—a conservative figure given that other estimates put the figure at about three years (*Business Week*, 1988) or even up to five years (Taylor & Standish, 1982). Thus, any euphoria on the part of users about a new system quickly turns to disenchantment due to the long delay before system delivery. Given this time-span for development, backlogs are inevitable. As already mentioned in Chapter 2, backlogs can be classified into two categories—a visible backlog and an invisible backlog. The visible backlog refers to the systems which have been formally requested and are scheduled for eventual development. However, many users, despairing at the size of the visible backlog, do not request systems that they may need, thus giving rise to an invisible backlog which is much larger than the visible one.

Thus, more rapid delivery of systems is needed, but the linear sequential phased approach of the traditional waterfall SDLC, which assumes that each individual phase can be satisfactorily completed before the next one begins, does not facilitate the rapid development of systems. All the phases in the SDLC should be completed in sequence as later phases depend on the successful completion of earlier phases. However, this requires "perfect foresight" (Henson & Hughes, 1991), since, for example, problems which may arise during physical design will have to be foreseen during the earlier logical design phase. Yet, perfect foresight is not facilitated by the SDLC in which phases are carried out more in the context of "imperfect predecessors" to use Taylor & Standish's (1982) term. The latter characterised the SDLC approach as follows:

> Because we live in an imperfect world, each of these (SDLC) activities usually takes place in the context of imperfect predecessors. That is, we live in a world where requirements are never likely to be complete or accurate, designs are never likely to be correct, and implementations are never likely to satisfy the requirements and reflect the design intentions perfectly.

Another major problem with the classical SDLC approach is that it rests on the *a priori* assumption that a complete and detailed understanding of the requirements of the problem situation can be achieved and that these requirements can be specified completely in advance, frozen, and a system designed and implemented based on these frozen specifications. However, it has been well established that users cannot specify their requirements completely in advance. Brooks (1987) has argued that the hardest part of systems development is determining the specifications of what to develop, and concludes that the assumption that requirements can be specified in advance is "fundamentally wrong." Parnas & Clements (1986) have also argued similarly, pointing out that users typically do not know their complete requirements, and that there is inevitable backtracking as development takes place.

It is the case that problems are dynamic and change as they are being solved. Davis *et al.* (1988) has described user needs as a "moving target" which are "constantly evolving", and it is therefore inappropriate to try freeze requirements in the specification phase. This attempt to finalise requirements before any development takes place does not occur in other disciplines. McCracken & Jackson (1981) considered the situation to be analogous to deciding all item purchases upon entry to a supermarket. They suggest that the waterfall life-cycle may have seemed appropriate in the past due to the complexity of system development, but that it actually perpetuated the failure to bridge the communication gap between user and analyst. Thus, although developers are primarily concerned with building systems that fulfil user needs, paradoxically, many of the methods discussed earlier, being based on the SDLC concept, may be at odds with this desire.

In early development approaches, requirements were generally specified in textual form, but this often resulted in requirements specifications which were long-winded and dull, and as a result users were not motivated to read these specifications and so were not in a position to validate them. To counter this, graphical representation techniques for requirements specification were incorporated in the belief that they would be easier to assimilate and understand, thus facilitating communication between users and developers. However, static graphical representations have deficiencies in that they fail to capture the dynamic nature of system requirements; nor do they allow users to formulate requirements based on any real experience with the system. This latter is a significant deficiency in that it is argued that requirements specification is a heuristic or learning process which greatly benefits from the deeper insight that both developers and users get from realistic experience with an actual system. Users may not be able to specify in advance exactly what they want in a system but are able to recognise it when they see it—an example of a well-known psychological phenomenon, namely, that recognition is a far easier process than recall.

Further compounding the problem is the fact that errors in requirements which are not identified before coding or implementation are extremely costly to correct (Boehm, 1981; DeMarco, 1978). Thus, the problem of correctly determining user requirements is of central importance for systems development.

4.2.1   Defining Prototyping

Drawing from parallels in other disciplines, the approach which has been recommended to address the problems discussed above is that of prototyping. The latter is an essential facilitator in the rapid delivery of systems and suited to determining system requirements more completely and accurately. However, like many concepts in the software field, there is a lack of consensus on what prototyping is or should be. Vonk (1990, p. 20–22) defined the concepts prototype and prototyping respectively as:

> *(a prototype is) a working model of (parts of) an information systems, which emphasises specific aspects of that system.*

> *(prototyping is) an approach for establishing a systems requirements definition which is characterised by a high degree of iteration, by a very high degree of user participation in the development process and by an extensive use of prototypes.*

In this definition, prototyping is viewed as an approach for requirements definition, not a development approach. However, other researchers, such as Alavi (1984) have proposed a more expansive definition of prototyping which emphasises its wider role in system construction:

> *A prototype is an early version of the system that exhibits the essential features of the later operational system. Some ... prototypes may evolve into the actual production systems whereas others are used only for experimentation and may eventually be replaced by the production system.*

At any rate, prototyping emphasises a quick response to loosely specified needs, rather than the precise initial specification of requirements of the conventional SDLC approach. It is fundamentally about an iterative process of demonstration, review, refinement and expansion, and because this process is central, the verb 'prototyping' is more relevant and widely used than the noun 'prototype'.

4.2.2   Benefits and Weaknesses of Prototyping

Prototyping provides a number of benefits in the development process, by no means all of which are related to requirements definition, thus giving credence to the expanded view of the role of prototyping in systems development. Among the benefits cited are the following:

- In terms of requirements specification, prototyping is widely recognised as facilitating the specification of system requirements with greater precision, thus allowing for validation before continuing with later development stages. Each successive prototype forms a closer approximation of the requirements.
- In traditional development approaches, users play a somewhat passive role, whereas prototyping helps to increase user participation and commitment, which should lead to increased user acceptance of the system.
- Researchers have also suggested that prototyping elicits an "unusual sense of excitement and anticipation ... among users" (Berrisford & Wetherbe, 1979). They participate more freely and developers achieve better communication and establish greater rapport with users. This is also facilitated by the fact that prototyping reduces the adversarial nature of the specification sign-off.
- Prototyping is real and hands-on, rather than a review of an abstract specification. This helps to deepen the insight and learning process for both developers and users, and, in this manner, new requirements come to light thus ensuring a more complete specification of requirements. It also ensures that any proposed design is evaluated in a realistic context, a fundamental principle of good design according to Alexander (1964).

- Systems quality should be improved, in that requirements are more complete and users are satisfied and are less likely to request immediate modifications to systems when they are delivered.
- Because system functioning can be demonstrated very quickly, systems *appear* to be developed more quickly. However, there is real substance to such a claim, given that many design errors may be eliminated in the first place.

However, researchers have also identified a number of weaknesses in the prototyping approach, including the following:

- Managing a prototyping development project may be more difficult than managing a project undertaken with a conventional development approach, since the latter has the built in 'comfort' factors of clearly prescribed phases with milestones and specific deliverables.
- Prototyping may require the acquisition of expensive, unfamiliar software. Also, prototyping could potentially lead to a waste of considerable time and money, in that if the prototype is untimely or inappropriate, the development team may have expended considerable resources and may not have made any real progress in developing a system.
- Rapid prototyping may result in failure to develop an overall systems plan which can lead to problems with systems integration.
- When following a prototyping approach, the original business problem may not be thoroughly studied and too little time may be devoted to generating and evaluating alternative solutions. The temptation may be to begin with the requirements the users want most and develop the system 'out from that corner' which can lead to poorly structured systems.
- Prototyping may be oversold and rapid delivery of prototype systems may create unrealistic expectations among users as to the time-scale for developing fully-functional production systems.
- Prototyping may be difficult to apply on large systems development projects where it is not clear how the system should be divided for the purpose of prototyping.
- Prototyping requires a significant commitment on the part of users and it may be difficult to maintain user enthusiasm beyond the initial specification of high-priority requirements.

Prototyping is both a technique and a philosophy for systems development. Prototyping has been going on in practice for quite a long time, both formally and informally. Even those systems developed using a conventional life-cycle approach might be more properly considered as prototypes, but just having a longer cycle-time, particularly if we consider each release or version of the system to be a model of the ultimate system. Indeed, popular methods, such as SSADM, for example, (discussed above) have evolved to incorporate iterative prototyping concepts. As Taylor & Standish (1982) concluded: "prototyping may well be like democracy—flawed, but far better than the available alternatives".

4.3   EVOLUTIONARY AND INCREMENTAL DEVELOPMENT

Any attempt to clarify the issues discussed in the previous section is not made easier by the fact that different terms are used more or less synonymously with prototyping in the literature. Vonk (1990) differentiated between prototyping and what he terms the related concepts of evolutionary development, incremental development and participative development. Evolutionary and incremental development are discussed here, and participative development is discussed in the next section.

4.3.1   Evolutionary Development

According to Vonk, evolutionary development is concerned with the quick realisation of successive versions of the production system itself, while prototyping involves the development of prototypes of parts of the eventual production system. Vonk concluded that prototyping and evolutionary development cannot be combined since prototyping is fundamentally about iterating through approximations of system requirements until a stable definition is reached, whereas evolutionary development assumes that requirements will constantly change and, therefore, the iterative process never ends. In the evolutionary approach, a system is constructed which meets the requirements to the extent to which they are known. This initial version of the system is delivered to its intended users and is used to help clarify and refine further requirements which are then incorporated in subsequent versions of the system.

4.3.2   Incremental Development

Vonk also identified incremental development as a distinct approach in its own right. In this approach, the system as a whole is built up step by step, as successive versions deliver the previous version unchanged plus a number of new functions. In evolutionary development, on the other hand, a new version of the whole system is created each time as requirements become clearer, and these refined requirements are incorporated into each system version. The incremental approach implies that most of the requirements are known, but an incremental delivery is chosen, possibly to provide some initial capability at reduced cost by providing a usable subset of the overall system which can be made available to users quickly, rather than having them wait for the complete system.

4.4   PARTICIPATIVE DEVELOPMENT

Vonk suggested that participative development has also been confused with prototyping (cf. Hirschheim, 1983). Participative development is characterised by a high degree of user involvement in the development process—an integral feature of the prototyping approach also, and indeed, several researchers have indicated that prototyping should complement a participative approach (Dearnley & Mayhew, 1983). However, while user participation may be a necessary condition for prototyping, it is not sufficient, as a high degree of iteration and extensive use of prototypes are also essential features of the prototyping approach.

The concept of participation can be traced back to the early Greeks where it was associated with a democratic form of decision taking. Mumford (1984) suggested that participation is increasingly becoming a societal value which is recognised as morally right and conducive to a healthy community. Indeed, in some Scandinavian countries, the rights of workers to participate and influence changes in their work environment has long been enshrined in law (Land *et al.*, 1980). The concept, while not new, was quite late in its emergence in the ISD area. However, the rationale behind its emergence in this area was broadly twofold. Firstly, there was a recognition that it is ethically and morally right that workers should be heavily involved in the development of systems that are part of their working lives. In addition, it was recognised that traditional approaches had not been working well, and that participation could help address some of the problems. For example, change is an inherent part of modern organisations, but groups who are passive recipients of change may be more likely to fear and resist it (Mumford, 1984). Participation in the system development process should help to make users feel more involved and thus more committed and positive about the system.

Friedman (1989) traced the rise to prominence of the participation concept, describing the scenario of DP departments, whose values, working practices, and salaries came to be out of line with the rest of the organisation, thus leading to increased isolation of DP personnel as technical specialists. However, as mentioned earlier, systems are increasingly being aimed for more complex and less well-defined areas. Thus, technical developers are not really in a position to ensure that these systems precisely meet the needs of users without the participation and contribution of the latter. Also, technical development experts are in scarce supply and there is a need to leverage their expertise better. The participative approach achieves this by altering the balance of power so that technical developers become less the "doers" and more "advisors" or "facilitators." Mumford (1984, p. 103) captured the essence of this two stranded rationale:

> Participation is viewed both pragmatically and ideologically—something that helps efficiency, satisfaction and progress but which is also morally right.

Some of the benefits of participation have already been introduced above in discussing the rationale behind its emergence. Briefly, they include the following:

- There is a better leverage of technical staff resources as the balance of power is altered through the redistribution of tasks between developers and users. This allows technical experts to advise and facilitate, and the increased user involvement leads to more informed design decisions.
- Users are more in control of their own destiny and are less likely to resist change through fear or ignorance of its implications.
- There is often a culture clash between developers and users, but participation can lead to better and more effective communication and interaction between these groups.
- Participants report an increase in job satisfaction, performing a more diverse range of tasks and having greater latitude in decision making.
- Systems are rated as easier to operate and are more likely to be accepted by users.
- Staff reduction and redeployment become possible due to the extra predictability and visibility afforded into the development process and its likely progression.

However, a number of potential problems have also been identified with the participative approach:

- Development times may actually increase when a participative approach is used. However, empirical research carried out by Hirschheim (1985) suggests that delays typically occur in the design phase, but these could well be offset by a trouble-free implementation later.
- The development team may face industrial relations issues which they are not empowered to resolve. This means that top management intervention and support is likely to be necessary if the participation is to be successful.
- It may prove difficult to schedule design group sessions for users and developers, given the time constraints that relevant individuals may operate under.
- The process may be politically problematic. For example, developers may resist participation because they see it as encroaching on their traditional skill base, while users may also feel that systems development issues are not properly part of their job.

Several development approaches and methods have been proposed to cater for increased user participation, including ETHICS (Mumford & Weir, 1979), ISAC (Lundeberg, 1982) and PORGI (Oppelland, 1984).

The literature on the participative approach is generally positive, although most of the reports are based more on intuitive rather than empirical grounds. The participative approach attempts to enlarge the scope of systems design to include technical and social factors, both recognised as being very important. In the past, systems may have been developed which were technically feasible, but may have been rejected by users as not being appropriate to their needs for a variety of social reasons. This enlarged scope to consider the social dimension is central to the 'softer' approaches to systems development which are discussed later in this chapter.

4.5   RAPID APPLICATION DEVELOPMENT

The term Rapid Application Development (RAD) was introduced in the literature by James Martin in his 1991 book (Martin, 1991). Martin drew on the development experiences of Scott Shultz at the Dupont corporation in 1984. Shultz described a particular development approach, Rapid Interactive Production Prototyping (RIPP), which was clearly the forerunner to the RAD approach proposed by Martin. Earlier antecedents in the literature include that of Gane (1989). However, as illustrated by its emergence in actual development practice, it is a concept which has resonances for practitioners.

At first glance, RAD might be dismissed since it does not offer anything radically new in terms of tools or techniques. However, the real potential of RAD arises from the synthesis of currently-available tools and techniques, coupled with fundamentally different management principles that serve to overcome bureaucratic obstacles to faster development. Thus, the mission of RAD is the simple but powerful one of increasing development speed at a reduced cost without sacrificing quality.

4.5.1   Fundamental Principles Underpinning RAD

It is probably inevitable that definitions are elusive with any emerging concept that is being shaped through practical experiences, and RAD is no exception. Definitions vary in terms of it being characterised as a tool, method or lifecycle (cf. Baum, 1992; Card, 1995; Mimno, 1991). Given this definitional quagmire, the approach taken here is to document the fundamental primary principles underpinning RAD, thus allowing a clearer picture of the concept to coalesce. These principles include active user involvement, small empowered teams, frequent delivery of products which focus primarily on satisfaction of business functionality, iterative incremental development, top-down approach, and the use of integrated CASE wherever possible. These principles are complementary in many respects, and as a whole are extremely powerful. They are discussed in turn below:

Active User Involvement

The schism between users and developers in traditional development approaches has rightly been condemned—indeed, it is almost an axiom that user involvement is necessary for successful development. However, several studies have found that user involvement is not a simple issue, and the link between involvement and success is not a simple one (cf. Butler & Fitzgerald, 1998). The RAD approach recognises that user involvement is necessary for intellectual reasons—to reduce costly requirements elicitation problems, for example—and for political reasons—users may reject systems outright if they have not been sufficiently involved in development. However, the RAD operationalisation of the user involvement concept is a very rich one. At the heart of the RAD approach are joint application design (JAD) and joint requirements planning (JRP) workshops. These are extremely intensive sessions of short duration which serve to identify more completely problematic requirements analysis and systems design issues. All relevant parties are co-located thus leading to synchronisation in the communication process. Also, RAD recognises that users are not homogeneous and identifies a number of different roles that users may play. This emphasis on development roles is an important feature of the eXtreme Programming approach also, which will be discussed in the next section.

Small Empowered Teams

Again, the concept of development teams is not a new one. However focusing on each of the words, *small*, *empowered* and *teams* in turn, the advantages which accrue can be seen to be considerable. Firstly, communication channels increase exponentially in relation to team size. Thus, *small* team size ensures that the potential for communication distortion and conflict is kept to a minimum. Secondly, the *empowerment* element helps ensure that bureaucratic delays and shirking of decision-making responsibility, so inherently characteristic of the traditional requirements signoff, are minimised. Teams are empowered to make vital design decisions (although changes are reversible—an issue which is discussed again below). Finally, the *team* aspect serves to ensure that all the vital skills for successful development are present. As already mentioned the team issue has already been proven to be useful. For example, the Chief Programmer Team (CPT) under Harlan Mills which developed the New York Times system achieved incredible results—83,000 lines of code written in 22 months; after implementation, the system ran for 20 months before the first error occurred (cf. Baker, 1972; Mills, 1971; Yourdon, 1979). Successful development requires that many varied roles be accommodated, e.g. project manager, technical co-ordinator, developer, tester, scribe, user, executive sponsor. The fulfilment of these roles is facilitated by team composition, and their importance has been acknowledged by Microsoft who organise their software development around various development roles in a similar manner (Sinha, 1997).

Frequent Delivery of Products

As already mentioned, traditional development projects can take from 18 months to five years to complete—an issue increasingly problematic given the rapidly-changing nature of today's competitive market-place. RAD, by definition, seeks to reduce development time-spans. Thus, shorter time-boxes for development—typically 90 days—are an important feature. These shorter time-boxes make project management more straightforward in that it is easier to focus on necessary activities, and be more accurate as to what can be achieved. Also, this principle is concerned with delivery of *products*. Rather than being focused on *process* (see Section 4.9 on Software Process Improvement below), RAD is premised on delivering products which satisfy the essential criterion of addressing some business function.

Iterative Incremental Development

Another fundamental principle of RAD is that systems evolve incrementally and are never complete. Rather, new requirements emerge which are then built into the system. Thus, systems emerge through iterative prototyping, with iteration seen as useful and necessary, not as re-work delaying development. It is recognised that requirements specification is a heuristic or learning process which greatly benefits from the deeper insight that both developers and users get from realistic experience with an actual prototype system. Users may not be able to specify in advance exactly what they want in a system but are able to recognise it when they see it—an example of a well-known psychological phenomenon, namely, that recognition is a far easier process than recall. In traditional development, errors in requirements which are not identified before coding or implementation are extremely costly to correct (Boehm, 1981; DeMarco, 1978). In fact, it is now commonly accepted that since the system produced by the traditional life-cycle undergoes a significant maintenance phase, it may be more properly viewed as a prototype anyway.

RAD approaches often follow a truncated version of the SDLC, including, for example, only the stages of planning, design, development, and cut-over, with much iteration between the phases. Fig. 4.2 illustrates the effect of iterative development and prototyping on the life cycle. Typically the planning phase is only performed once at the initiation of the development project. Analysis, design coding and implementation are iterated in several 'chunks' or time-boxes. The maintenance activity grows as more and more of the system is developed, as indicated by the growing size of the maintenance component in Fig. 4.2.

Top-Down Approach

As already mentioned, the RAD philosophy accepts that requirements cannot be completely specified in advance. Rather, they are specified at a level appropriate to the knowledge available at the given time. These are then elaborated through incremental prototyping. Similarly, products fit for business purpose are produced

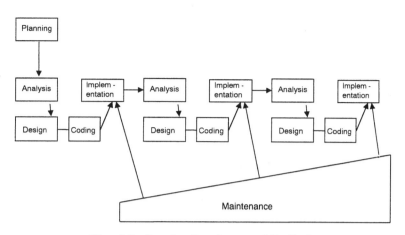

Fig. 4.2   Iterative Development Life Cycle

according to an application of the Pareto principle—that is, approximately 80 per cent of the functionality may be delivered in 20 per cent of the time. Systems are then elaborated and finessed as knowledge grows, from broad outline to precise detail. Also, being a top-down approach characterised by short time-boxing, all decisions are assumed to be fairly quickly reversible. This also contributes to developers feeling more empowered to assume responsibility and being less likely to shirk decision-making.

Integrated Computer Assisted Software Engineering (I-CASE)

If dramatic increases in development productivity are to be achieved, it is vital that the more routine and time-consuming aspects of development be automated. These include code generation and documentation, for example. The automation of these tasks may be achieved through the use of I-CASE. The latter provides a single electronic repository for project-related data. Change control and configuration management features—vital in an environment of iterative prototyping—are also provided. Additionally, I-CASE facilitates reuse by providing access to previously designed and tested elements. Thus, by increasing the granularity of the development building block, productivity improvement is further enhanced.

4.5.2   The DSDM RAD Method

A RAD method which is of especial interest to us is the Dynmaic Systems Development Method (DSDM), produced by a consortium of the same name. The primary reason for our interest is because it is a method which has been inductively derived from actual development practice in a large number of organisations. The DSDM consortium originated with 16 founding member organisations who met in January

1994 with the goal of creating a standard RAD method for the consortium. Version 1 of the DSDM RAD method was completed on time (not surprisingly perhaps!), to unanimous member agreement and published in February 1995. Coinciding with this, a training scheme was initiated, and an examination procedure for DSDM practitioners to gain certification was instigated in co-operation with the British Computer Society. Following further practical validation through an Early Adopters Programme, Version 2 was published ahead of schedule in December 1995. Version 3, published in October 1997, involved refinements to the method to shift its focus from purely application development to also cater for business process reengineering projects—the latter being very much in vogue in organisations in the mid to late 1990s.

The method is continuously evolving through White Papers and other case studies and experience reports—the link between DSDM and the Unified Modelling Language (UML) (see the section on the Rational Unified Process below) is covered in a White Paper, for example. The method is very well supported by a comprehensive web site (www.dsdm.org). There are currently more than 400 European organisations in the consortium. Version 4 of the method is due for general release in early 2002, and, in addition to fine-tuning many of the existing techniques and processes within DSDM, it will also place more emphasis on the role of testing, and also the importance of method tailoring (the method tailoring issue discussed in more detail in Chapter 9). This latter aspect also brings the DSDM method very much into a method-in-action category.

According to the documentation on the DSDM web site (www.dsdm.org) at the time of writing, the method comprises the following five generic stages, which are tailored to the specific business and technical needs of the development context:

- Feasibility Study
- Business study
- Functional model iteration
- Design and build iteration
- Implementation

These stages follow a spiral life-cycle as depicted in Fig 4.3.

Feasibility Study

In this phase, the focus of concern is whether the proposed development will actually meet the business needs, whether the DSDM method is even suitable for the project, and an estimate of the development time-scale and costs, and a rough project plan is produced. This phase should occupy a few weeks at most.

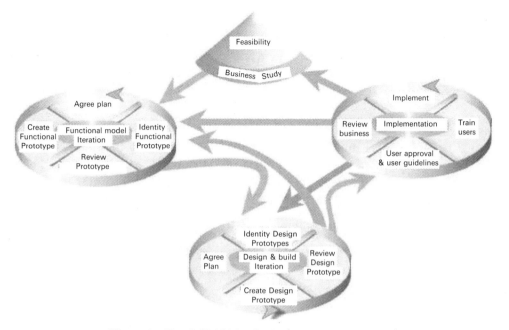

Fig. 4.3   The DSDM Life Cycle (from www.dsdm.org)

Business Study

This phase identifies the scope of the overall project and provides a sound business and technical basis for all future work. High-level functional and non-functional requirements are base-lined, a high-level model of the business functionality and informational requirements is produced, the system architecture is outlined and the maintainability objectives are agreed. Like the feasibility study, the business study is a short phase, of no more than a month.

The Feasibility and Business Studies are done sequentially and set the ground rules for the rest of the development; therefore, they must be completed before any work is carried out on a given project.

Functional Model Iteration

In this phase, the focus is on refining the business aspects of the system, that is, building on the high-level functional and informational requirements. This phase consists of cycles of four activities:

- Identify what is to be produced
- Agree how and when to do it
- Create the product
- Check that it has been produced correctly

It is estimated that the bulk of development work is in the two iteration phases where prototypes are incrementally built towards the tested system. All prototypes in DSDM are intended to evolve into the final system and are therefore built to be robust enough for operational use and to satisfy any relevant non-functional requirements, such as performance.

Design and Build Iteration

During the Design And Build iteration, the focus is on ensuring that the system is of sufficiently high standard to be safely put into production. The major product here is the tested system. The lifecycle does not show testing as a distinct activity because testing is happening throughout both the functional model iteration and design and build iteration. The tested system will satisfy all the agreed requirements, that is the essential requirements plus as many others as the time available allows. This phase comprises the same cycle of four activities as the previous phase, Functional Model Iteration.

Implementation

The implementation phase covers the transfer from the development environment to the operational environment. This includes training all users and handing over the system to them. The project review document is also produced and summarises what the project has achieved. It reviews all the requirements, which were identified during development and the position of the system in relation to those requirements. Because DSDM is incremental there are four possible outcomes:

- Everything was delivered and there is no need for further development (hence no arrow in Fig 4.3).
- A new functional area was discovered during development and development returns to the business study phase.
- A less essential part of the functionality was missed out due to time con-straints. Development returns to the start of the functional model iteration and adds the functionality to the delivered system.
- A non-functional requirement has not been satisfied and development returns to the design and build iteration to rectify this.

4.5.3   Summary of RAD

Thus, it can be seen that RAD is an approach that is addressing some of the same issues as prototyping, iterative/evolutionary development, and participative approaches. Specific RAD methods include James Martin's RAD (Martin, 1991) and the aforementioned Dynamic Systems Development Method (DSDM, 1995).

RAD offers the advantages of speed, lower cost, closer ties between requirements, specifications, and the finished product (due to the shortened, iterative life cycle), and user involvement. Problems can occur, however, when controls are omitted, systems are developed in isolation and are not integrated with other systems, and when there is a lack of standardisation. These problems are more likely to occur when RAD is used to develop systems outside of the formal IS function.

Tools used in RAD include prototyping, Joint Application Design, and automated development tools (CASE tools) providing screen and report designing and code generation facilities. Joint Application Design sessions bring together developers and users to make design decisions. Often these sessions are held in special technology-equipped meeting rooms to allow the actual creation of design documents and prototypes in real time.

Beynon-Davies *et al.* (1997) note that while much has been written on the concept of RAD, there remains a paucity of empirical studies which have investigated the RAD phenomenon in actual practice. The work of the aforementioned authors represents a notable effort in redressing this imbalance (Beynon-Davies *et al.*, 1997, 1998), as does the DSDM method discussed above. However, much remains to be done to elaborate the RAD concept. Problems may be anticipated in the areas of management and control, raised user expectations, half-hearted implementation of the concept, and so on. Also, the issue of RAD suitability—that is, whether it is appropriate for use in the development of safety-critical systems—needs to be further investigated. Indeed, it may be the case that traditional development approaches may be more appropriate in some circumstances. Clearly, more empirical studies of the concept, as advocated by Beynon-Davies *et al.* (1998), are necessary.

4.6   EXTREME PROGRAMMING (XP)

The eXtreme Programming (XP) approach to development shares many similarities with the RAD approach, in so far as it acknowledges that it is not a magic 'silver bullet' of revolutionary new techniques; rather, it is a set of tried and trusted principles which are well-established as part of the conventional wisdom of software engineering, but which are taken to an extreme level—hence the name eXtreme Programming. In a similar fashion, RAD is also an amalgam of existing tools and management processes configured in a new mission as discussed above. Also, open source software, which will be discussed later, both in this chapter and again in Chapter 10, is often promoted as a radical change in software development, but at its heart it is based on some fundamental principles of software engineering.

XP has been pioneered by Kent Beck and is comprehensively described in Beck (2000), where he describes it as "a light-weight methodology for small-to-medium-sized teams developing software in the face of vague or rapidly-changing requirements." The method comprises 12 key practices, summarised in Table 4.1.

The Planning Game
A quick determination of the scope of the next software release, based on a combination of business priorities and technical estimates. It is accepted that this plan will probably change.

Small releases
Put a simple system into production quickly, then release new versions on a very short cycle.

Metaphor
Guide all development with a simple shared story of how the whole system works.

Simple design
The system should be designed as simply as possible at any given moment in time.

Testing
Programmers continually write tests which must be run flawlessly for development to proceed. Customers write function tests to demonstrate the features implemented.

Refactoring
Programmers restructure the system, without removing functionality, to improve non-functional aspects (e.g. duplication of code, simplicity, flexibility).

Pair programming
All production code is written by two programmers at one machine.

Collective ownership
Anyone can change any code anywhere in the system at any time.

Continuous integration
Integrate and build the system every time a task is completed—this may be many times per day.

40-hour week
Work no more than 40 hours per week as a rule.

On-site customers
Include an actual user on the team, available full-time to answer questions.

Coding standards
Adherence to coding rules which emphasise communication via program code.

Table 4.1   Key Practices of XP (from Beck, 2000)

4.6.1   Key Practices of XP

The Planning Game

This practice strives to determine the project scope and achieve a balance between business and technical considerations. The business aspects that need to be decided are the project scope, prioritisation of the most important functionality for initial development, and realistic dates for releases of the system from a business point of view.

The technical aspects which need to be determined include estimates of time to implement various features, and how the development process will be organised.

Small Releases

Each release should be as small as possible while still containing a coherent set of business requirements. Generally short time-boxes of one or two months are preferable to six months or a year.

Metaphor

Ideally, each XP project should have a single overarching metaphor. The metaphor helps project participants understand the basic elements and their relationships. In conventional system development, the term 'architecture' is sometimes used as an alternative, but Beck argues that a metaphor can provide a better sense of cohesion. Metaphors can range from very naÿve simplistic system names, such as a 'contract management system,' to richer metaphors such as 'computer as desktop' or 'system as a spreadsheet.'

Simple Design

This is an instantiation of Einstein's maxim that *everything in life should be as simple as possible but no simpler*. In XP it is expected that every aspect of the system design can be justified at that moment in time. As Beck (p. 57) puts it: "put in what you need when you need it." His basic argument is that in conventional development, extra functionality is often added on the presumption that it might be needed in the future. However, as a consequence the design may become overly complicated.

Testing

Testing is accorded extreme importance in XP, to the extent that it becomes 'test-first' programming. That is, one should write a test before writing code, and all code undergoes exhaustive testing as soon as it is written. There are two key categories of testing: unit tests which are written by the programmers to ensure the code works, and function tests which are written by the customers to ensure the system meets the business requirements.

Refactoring

The refactoring concept is discussed in detail in Fowler (1999). Basically, it involves making changes to a system which do not affect its functional behaviour, but which enhance some non-functional quality such as simplicity, flexibility, understandability, performance. It is quite closely related to the *Simple Design* practice.

Pair Programming

One of the more novel and apparently extreme practices of XP is that of pair programming. Basically, this involves all production code being written by two people using just one computer. The idea is that each individual performs complementary roles. For example, while one is coding, the other might be constructing tests, or considering more high-level strategic issues. Also, when courage is needed to undertake some of the bolder XP practices, a pair is less likely to shirk responsibility.

Collective Ownership

In the early days of programming, there was no such thing as code ownership—anyone could change anything to suit their own immediate needs. This resulted in chaos as programs were heavily inter-coupled, and changes were made in an undisciplined manner. As a consequence, individual code ownership became the norm. In this model, only the official owner of the code was entitled to change it. While this model resulted in more stability, it caused much inertia and meant that systems were not sufficiently responsive to necessary code changes. In XP, all programmers should know enough about the system to make any necessary changes to improve code.

Continuous Integration

Code is integrated into the whole release and tested every few hours ideally, or after a day of development at the outside. Programmers load the latest release, load their changes, and run the tests until they pass 100 per cent. This ensures that the responsibility for fixing errors is always obvious, as code is not integrated unless it is working 100 per cent.

40-Hour Week

While the amount of productive work that can be done per week varies among different individuals, sustained overtime, even to the point of working overtime two weeks in a row, is seen as symptomatic of more serious fundamental problems on the project. Programmers cannot be expected to be fresh and productive if they are working overtime on a regular basis. This obviously is at odds with the tales of heroics and prodigious feats of coding common in the software folklore.

On-Site Customer

A real customer should be available to the team on a full-time basis to answer questions, resolve disputes and set small scale priorities. The customer should be located directly with the XP team. This is expected to be problematic as organisations may be reluctant to spare someone to serve in such a capacity. However, it is probably feasible that a customer playing such a role could perform some of their normal work, albeit not directly located in their normal workplace.

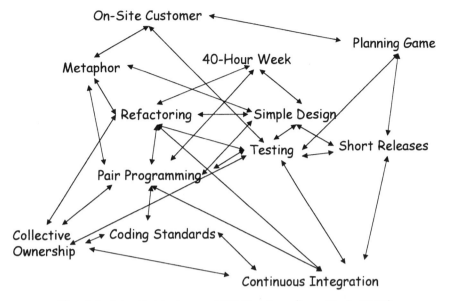

Fig. 4.4   Inter-Relatedness of XP Practices (from Beck, 2000)

Coding Standards

The collective ownership practice means that any programmer can make changes to any code at any time. Also, refactoring can result in the same outcome. Given this situation, it is vital that generally accepted coding standards be enacted and adhered to.

4.6.2   Summary of XP

A marked feature of XP is that several of the practices overlap to some extent and thus serve to complement and reinforce each other—refactoring, simple design, collective ownership and coding standards, for example. The inter-relatedness of the practices is depicted graphically in Fig. 4.4.

One of the reasons that XP is of especial interest to us is because it again is an approach that has been derived and refined from the lessons of actual development practice. As already mentioned, a weakness of many formalised ISD methods is that they are proposed on the basis of what should theoretically work, and are not subsequently 'tested' to ensure they work in real development situations (see Chapter 3). Another reason for our interest in XP is that it is very much a method-in-action. Beck emphasises this on several occasions. For example:

> *In adopting each practice, you will shape it to your situation (p. 123). (XP) is idealized ... no two XP projects could (or should) ever be exactly alike (p. 131)*

Another principle that we hold dear is that developers are a critical component in ISD. This was discussed in Chapter 2 above and, later, Chapter 7 is devoted entirely to developer-related issues. XP is also very much a people-centred approach—"the programmer is the heart of XP" as Beck terms it (p. 141), and he also recognises the central role of the customer—"the driver of a software project is the customer" (p. 28). Also, when summarising the various development roles that arise in XP, he is equally forthright on the issue:

> *If you have people who don't fit the roles, change the roles. Don't try to change the people (p. 140).*

Beck also acknowledges that XP is not a 'one size fits all' phenomenon, and that is not suited to all projects. For example:

- Organisational culture is a critical component. XP requires a fresh mind and the constant overtime that is a feature of many modern software organisations is anathema to XP.
- Organisations who are wed to the traditional mode of performing a thorough analysis to produce a complete set of requirements specifications prior to doing any work on design and coding will not be able to implement an XP approach.
- XP is not a development approach that is suited to development teams larger than twenty developers.
- On certain computing platforms where interoperability requires code to be excessively complex, XP is not suited, as it is an approach premised around keeping the code as clean and simple as possible.
- Where system compilation and integration take a long time, the prompt feedback principle of XP is contravened, and thus such systems are not appropriate for an XP approach.
- In certain environments, software testing is very difficult if not impossible. For example, the computing architecture could be prohibitively expensive or spare capacity to facilitate testing might not be available. Testing is a *sine qua non* for XP, and thus XP should not be adopted in such a context.
- The spatial configuration is also important for XP, as pair programming is an inherent feature, as is inter-team communication. Thus, an environment in which programmers and users are located in separate offices and even buildings is not conducive to an XP approach.

Overall, XP fits within a general trend towards RAD and lean and agile methods (cf. Highsmith, 2000; Highsmith & Cockburn, 2001; Poppendieck, 2001) which have emerged as a reaction to the cumbersome and long development time-scales associated with traditional ISD projects as discussed above. These methods emphasise agility and are people and product focused rather than being concerned with process discipline, as in the case of approaches such as the Capability Maturity Model (CMM) discussed later in this chapter.

4.7   THE RATIONAL UNIFIED PROCESS

The Rational Unified Process® is a commercial method developed and marketed by Rational, Inc., the same organisation that gave us the Unified Modelling Language (UML), which is discussed later in this section. By the end of 1999, more than one thousand organisations were using this method, including Ericsson, MCI, British Aerospace, Intel, and Oracle (Kruchten, 2000).

The origins of the Rational Unified Process (RUP) pre-date the merger of Rational Software Corporation and Objectory AB in 1995. This merger brought together two existing processes, the Rational Approach with its focus on iterative development and architecture, and the Objectory process version 3.8, which incorporated process models and use cases, created in 1987 by Ivar Jacobson. This iteration, which appeared in 1996, was called Rational Objectory Process 4.0. This version of the process was the first to use the newly created Unified Modelling Language (Krutchen, 2000). The next version, 4.1, which came out only one year later, included additions acquired when other companies merged with Rational. Among these were detailed test processes from SQA, Inc. and requirements management from Requisite, Inc.

The Rational Unified Process 5.0 was introduced in 1998. Along with the new name came a number of additions, including business engineering, configuration and change management, data engineering, and user interface design. Since that time, real-time and web-based development components have been added, and RUP continues to evolve.

4.7.1   Key Components of RUP

Whereas the Rational Unified Process has evolved from object-oriented methods, it is considered to be more than a systems development method. RUP is described as a "software engineering process" and a "configurable process framework," referring to the fact that it can be modified to accommodate the specific needs, characteristics, constraints, and history of the organisation, culture, and domain in which it is used. In other words, the development method itself can be customised to fit a particular development context. Configuration criteria include the business context—whether the system is being developed for internal use, for a client, or for commercial sale—the size of the project, the degree of novelty, and the type of application being

Best Practice	**Implemented in RUP through:**
Develop software iteratively	Frequent executable releases
Manage requirements	Use cases to capture functional requirements
Use component-based architectures	Architecture definition using components
Model software visually	Unified Modelling Language
Verify software quality continuously	Testing throughout lifecycle
Control changes to software	Isolating changes; procedures

Table 4.2   Best Practices as Implemented in RUP

developed (Krutchen, 1996). This tailoring of the process is done by modifying, customising, adding or suppressing particular components of the process.

The Rational Unified Process implements 'best practices' identified as processes commonly used by successful system development organisations. These are defined in Table 4.2.

At the heart of the Rational Unified Process is the use case. A use case diagram represents in a simple pictorial format the functions of the system and the external entities (actors) that interact with the system. Each use case represents one view of the system. A set of use cases is typically required to represent all the functionality of a system. Narrative use case descriptions supplement the diagrams and provide more detail regarding issues such as timing and control. Use cases provide a consistent, visible thread through the system model by defining the behaviour performed by the system.

RUP is represented using a two-dimension model, with time on the horizontal axis and the content dimension on the vertical axis. (See Fig. 4.5) The four phases in the time dimension are inception, elaboration, construction, and transition. The system is developed iteratively. Each iteration includes requirements, design, implementation and assessment activities, and results in an executable process that represents one generation of the system. The vertical access represents the core workflows or activities in the RUP. Whereas the core process workflows of business modelling, requirements, analysis and design, implementation, testing, and deployment appear the same as the sequential phases of a traditional waterfall process, in the iterative method "these workflows are revisited again and again throughout the lifecycle" (Rational, 1998). Supporting workflows are used throughout the lifecycle to manage and control the process. These model components are described in the following sections.

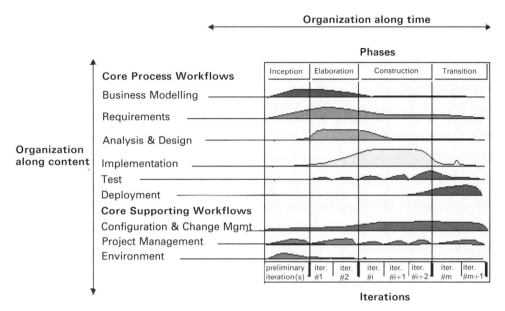

Fig. 4.5   The Iterative Model (from www.rational.com)

4.7.2   Phases of the Rational Unified Process

Inception

In the inception phase, the project scope is defined, feasibility is assessed, and a business case including a rough estimate of cost and time requirements, a set of success criteria, and a risk assessment are generated. To complete this, all external entities (actors) with which the system interacts are identified, and significant use cases are defined. Outcome of the inception phase may also include one or more initial prototypes of the system. To successfully complete this phase and move on to the next phase, stakeholder concurrence on scope and time/cost estimates is required.

Elaboration

Through a deeper analysis of the problem domain, the elaboration phase establishes the architectural foundation, develops the project plan, and structures the project in such as way so as to eliminate the highest risk elements. The use case model is extended to include all use cases and actors, and most use case descriptions are produced. A complete architectural prototype is developed, addressing at a minimum all the significant use cases identified in the inception phase. At the end of this phase, the decision is made whether or not to commit to the remainder of the development process.

Construction

The focus of the construction phase, as indicated by its name, is the building of the system, including fleshing out requirements, designing, coding and testing the system. In large projects, parallel construction activities can take place, which significantly speed up the deployment of new releases. At the end of the construction phase, it is decided if the system—not only the software, but also the hardware sites and users—is ready to go into operation. If not, the next phase, transition, is delayed until the readiness criteria are met.

Transition

In the transition phase the system is released to the users. Activities involved include validating the system against user expectations ('beta testing'), converting databases, training, and finally rolling-out the software product to all users. This phase is likely to involve several iterations, including the initial 'beta' releases, general availability releases, and releases correcting errors or containing enhancements.

4.7.3   Core Workflows of the Rational Unified Process

Business Modelling

The purpose of this workflow is to facilitate communication and coordination of the business and software development communities. Business use cases are created and used to understand how the system should support the business model.

Requirements

This workflow describes *what* the system is supposed to do. More specifically, actors are identified, stakeholder needs are determined, and use cases and use case descriptions are created to represent the major activities of the system. The use cases created here will carry through the rest of the lifecycle.

Analysis and Design

Using the results of the previous workflow, the analysis and design workflow results in a blueprint describing *how* the system will work. The design model created in this workflow includes the design for the components of the system as well as interfaces and interactions between them.

Implementation

In implementation, the design is turned into an executable system. In RUP, this is done by aggregating components, either through reuse of existing components or creation of new ones. The use of components and a modular architecture extends concepts of modularity and encapsulation from object-oriented design.

Testing

The Rational Unified Process incorporates iterative testing throughout the lifecycle. Testing examines three dimensions of quality: reliability, functionality, and performance of the application and the system (Rational, 1998). Testing is done at the end of each iteration and for each new release of the project.

Deployment

Deployment delivers the product (system) to the users. Although the majority of the activities related to deploying the system are done during the transition phase, some activities such as migration of data, training, and planning must be considered in earlier phases.

Supporting Workflows

The core supporting workflows of configuration and change management, project management, and environment are used across all phases of the lifecycle. These workflows address the overall management of the project: the allocation of resources, management of risk, version control, and development tools. The on-line support environment provides links to activities (tasks that must be performed) and to artefacts (deliverables).

4.7.4   The Unified Modelling Language and RUP

The Unified Modelling Language (UML) is an industry-standard graphical language for describing, constructing, and documenting system components (artefacts). UML was originally created by Rational Software (Booch *et al.*, 1998) and is now maintained by the Object Management Group, the main standards organisation for object-oriented issues (Stevens and Pooley, 2000).

UML includes nine diagram types. The use case diagram is considered by many to be the most important of the diagram types. Use case diagrams are used to model the functionality of systems and the interactions with external entities, called actors in UML. Use case diagrams form the foundation for the Rational Unified Process by providing a consistent thread throughout the iterations and phases of the lifecycle.

Class diagrams describe the structure of the system by identifying classes (including data and methods) and their relationships. An object diagram is a particular instantiation of the class diagram which describes the structure of the system at one particular point in time through the values associated with the data attributes.

Other diagrams include the sequence, collaboration, statechart, activity, component, and deployment diagrams. These diagrams model behaviour, control and resources. For more details and examples of these, see Rumbaugh *et al.* (1999).

Whereas UML is tightly interwoven into the Rational Unified Process and Rational's CASE tool, Rational Rose, it is not used exclusively with this process model or this tool. UML is popular independently as a modelling tool for object-oriented approaches. (See, for example, Mathiassen *et al.*, 2000).

4.7.5   Summary of the Rational Unified Process

The Rational Unified Process treats the software development process like software itself. The process is designed, developed, delivered and maintained. The process can be tailored and configured and integrated with other tools. The process is an on-line framework which provides tools such as mentors, templates, examples, and pre-configured variants on the basic process such as RUP for e-business (Krutchen, 2000).

The iterative approach embodied in RUP is particularly suitable for long, novel, and/or risky projects because each release is tested several times throughout the lifecycle. RUP advocates claim that it is applicable to projects of any size through the customisation and tailoring of the process. Regardless of the size of the system, because requirements are refined with users' input throughout the iterations, this process should result in a system that is more likely to meet their needs (Kutchen, 2000).

Whereas RUP provides a strategy for developing artefacts and deliverables, and also information on how to perform design and development tasks, it does not do a lot of processing itself. Instead it takes advantage of the on-line delivery model to provide access to a large body of information. RUP does not ensure a proper step-by-step process, nor does it enforce policies (Barnhart, 2001). However, this lack of rigidity can be viewed as an advantage. It is this flexibility that allows the broad variety of configurations of the process framework.

The Rational Unified Process is very much a method-in-action, tailored to fit the particular development context. The concept of method tailoring, and a specific industry example, are discussed in detail in Chapter 9.

4.8   'SOFT' APPROACHES TO IS DEVELOPMENT

The development approaches discussed up to now tended to consider systems development from the more technical or 'hard' scientific perspective, which had been a dominant influence in the field, evidenced by the following from Keen & Scott Morton (1978, p. 49):

> *(there is) a general sense that the central issues for MIS are technical and that the introduction of the computer into an organisation's operations is beneficial and inevitable.*

This bias has manifested itself in a stream of literature from the 1960s which focused on the 'software crisis' with expressions of concern about expenditure and poor productivity. As a consequence, the solutions which have been proposed have been essentially of a hard technical nature. This stream of literature has had a major effect on teaching and practice. However, another stream of literature which began at the same time was concerned with softer issues such as user relations, the rise of technocracy, and consequences of computer system malfunction (Friedman, 1989). This literature was generated by citizens' groups, novelists and film-makers, but it did not have the same profound effect as the first stream. However, since the 1980s, the literature on systems development and the literature on the implications of computing for users have been merging. This has led to a consideration of softer approaches to systems development.

It is recognised that the terms 'hard' and 'soft', which are used here, have not been defined. However, the terms are in common usage and do have intuitive meanings. To clarify the distinction between these terms, it is useful to view these as end points of a continuum and to consider some of the features and factors which characterise each end of the continuum.

At the hard end of the continuum, an ontological position of realism is adopted. The focus is primarily external and the existence of an objective empirical reality is assumed. At the hard end of the spectrum, an engineering approach to accomplishing tasks is taken, and people are seen in mechanistic terms as processing devices who undertake tasks that could be done by machine.

In extreme contrast, at the soft end of the continuum, the ontological dimension is the subjective nominalist one. The world is viewed as existing in people's minds; there is no independent verifiable reality as people can interpret things differently, and thus reality is socially constructed. People are central and there is an emphasis on achieving empathy and understanding. Also, there is a rejection of the notion of people as processors equivalent to machines in some respects; rather systems exist to support people. Avison *et al.* (1992, p. 274) clarified the difference between hard and soft systems thinking as follows:

(The) difference between hard and soft systems thinking is that in hard systems thinking a goal is assumed. The analyst modifies the system in some way so that a goal is achieved in the most efficient manner. The analysts identify a problem to be 'solved' and attempt to solve it. Hard systems thinking is concerned about the 'how' of the problem. In soft systems thinking, on the other hand, the objectives of the system are assumed to be more complex than a simple goal that can be achieved and measured. Understanding can be achieved through debate with all the 'actors' and emphasis is placed on the 'what' of the system. The analyst is not concerned with 'the' problem, but a situation in which problems exist—hence the term problem situation.

Several researchers have classified systems development approaches according to dimensions such as these (Downs *et al.*, 1992; Floyd, 1987; Hirschheim & Klein, 1989; Oliga, 1988). However, these researchers readily admit that such classifications are difficult and somewhat arbitrary in that development approaches do not occupy a single place on such a continuum.

Development approaches such as the traditional SDLC approach, the Structured Approach, and Information Engineering have been located at the hard end of the continuum by Hirschheim & Klein (1989) who characterised these approaches as follows:

> *Their application helps to make systems development more formal and rational, placing less reliance on human intuition, judgement and politics.*

Underpinning these approaches is the view that there exists a reality that is measurable and essentially the same for everyone. Hirschheim & Klein illustrated this in relation to the Structured Approach, citing McMenamin & Palmer's (1984, p. 77) contention that "the specification should contain all the true requirements and nothing but the true requirements".

SSADM may also be located at the hard end of the spectrum according to Downs *et al.* (1992) who stated that:

> *(SSADM) has strong links with the traditional structured methods. To the extent that there are choices of techniques and the structure may be modified, it is a contingency approach. However, the choices are amongst hard techniques.*

The other development approaches discussed earlier, such as JSD, are clearly from the hard end of the spectrum also.

However, the prototyping approach shifts the perspective away from the hard end somewhat according to Hirschheim & Klein, in its recognition of the importance of the user and the "subjective and emerging nature of requirements". They summarise it as follows:

> *In prototyping, users and analysts interact to construct a working model of the system which is then refined and modified in a continuous process, until the fit between user and system is acceptable.*

The introduction of concepts such as *user participation* and the incorporation of *human factors* into development methods caused a shift towards the softer end of the spectrum. However, even though acknowledging the role of users more, hard influences were still generally predominant. Downs *et al.* describe this in the SSADM method, saying:

> *The involvement of users in the development effort may be regarded as a step towards the soft end of the spectrum. However, these users need to express themselves in terms of the hard techniques, e.g. requirements must be written down (quantified and cost justified if at all possible).*

Bjorn-Andersen (1988) has argued that the incorporation of human factors is fundamentally limited in that a "narrow engineering approach" is still adopted with "the naive assumption that technology is neutral". Thus, the goal is to reduce the resistance to technology and the emphasis is on adapting technology to human weaknesses. Consequently, some of these efforts do not really move far from the hard end of the spectrum.

The soft approaches to systems development have primarily been associated with Scandinavia (a notable exception being SSM from the UK). It is worth noting however, that there are significant cultural differences between Scandinavian and US/UK society, for example. Floyd *et al.* (1989) in their outline of the background to Scandinavian approaches, refer to Scandinavian society with its emphasis on quality of life, worker participation, and the like. Other researchers in the area have also noted the differences between Scandinavian society and other societies. For example, Bjorn-Andersen (1988) reports an example of different advertising strategies for an office automation product in Scandinavia and the US. In the latter, the emphasis was on cost efficiency and ease of learning which served to reduce training costs. However, for the same product in Scandinavia, the emphasis was on creating a better work environment, eliminating routine work and creating more challenging jobs. Bjorn-Andersen links this difference, in part, to trade union influence in working practices which seek to eliminate the dehumanising and deskilling of work. Related to this, Friedman (1989) notes that the term 'user' in the US or UK context tends to mean managers of user departments, whereas in the Scandinavian context, it is generally intended to mean end-user staff in the user department, or even a union representative of the users, as the position of data steward—a full-time shop steward—is a common one in Scandinavian organisations.

Among the methods which adopt a 'soft' perspective, albeit to different degrees, are SSM (Checkland, 1981; Checkland & Scholes, 1990; Checkland, 1999), ISAC (Lundeberg, 1982), ETHICS (Mumford, 1983), PIOCO (Iivari & Koskela, 1987), Multiview (Wood-Harper *et al.*, 1985; Avison & Wood-Harper, 1990), Multiview2 (Avison *et al.*, 1998), MARS (Anderson & Matthiassen, 1987), UTOPIA (Howard, 1985), and SAMPO (Lehtinen & Lyytinen, 1984). In this section, SSM is discussed, as it is the most developed and widely disseminated variant of the soft approaches.

4.8.1   Soft Systems Methodology (SSM)

SSM introduced a radically different perspective into the field. SSM is a methodology that has had a substantial impact on the understanding and development of methods. Over the years SSM is probably one of the most referenced and cited approaches in ISD research, but despite this, it is not widely used outside academia. Peter Checkland, the creator of SSM, based soft systems methodology on two different arguments. The first argument was uncommon since it was strictly philosophical. It consisted of a broad and deep analysis of the underlying assumptions behind systems thinking and systems development. This led to an elaborated definition of the concept of systems and how systems are made up of humans and human activities.

The other argument was developed over a number of years. It was the outline of a practical approach, based on the philosophical understanding, derived experientially from the distillation of experiences in a large number of action research projects. It is fully documented in Checkland (1981), Wilson (1984), and a modified format in Checkland and Scholes (1990), Checkland (1999) and in numerous articles and papers.

Wilson (1984) has argued that SSM represents a paradigm shift for systems development in that most development methods are based upon the paradigm of optimisation whereas SSM adopts a learning paradigm which recognises "ill-structured (soft) problems to which there are no such thing as 'right', or optimised, answers". The SSM approach acknowledges the importance of people in an organisational context and attempts to make sense of complex human activity systems which are characterised by fuzzy or messy problem situations. The method allows the problem situation to be studied from many points of view, thus ensuring a better understanding of the complexities of the situation. The method also recognises that the analyst or developer cannot be neutral in his or her understanding of the studied system, but is governed by an inherent *weltanschauung*. The notion of *weltanschauung* plays an important role in SSM. It can be understood as the world view encompassing the assumptions and mind-set of the developer. SSM was one of the very first approaches to make this non-neutrality explicit. The methodology comprises a seven stage process which serves as a means of progressing through three levels, namely, finding out about the situation, systems thinking, and taking action (see Table 4.3).

The original seven-stage format of SSM has been modified on the basis of its application in a number of development projects (Checkland & Scholes, 1990). In their defence of the revised version, Checkland & Scholes state that SSM has mistakenly been viewed as a method for soft, ill-structured problems, rather than hard problems. They resolve the distinction between hard and soft by incorporating hard as a special case of soft.

Ethical, political and social issues have also been explicitly recognised and accorded a prominent role in the revised version of SSM. Also, two modes of use

Stages 1 and 2: Finding out

The first two stages are concerned with finding out about the problem situation. This involves creating a rich picture of the situation by whatever means possible. The rich picture contains details on significant processes, people taking part, communication lines, the environment, owners of the system, and problems and areas of conflict. Creating an acceptable rich picture may require several iterations but the process serves to stimulate debate and ensures a richer understanding of the problem situation than that achieved by conventional hard analysis techniques.

Stage 3: Selection

This stage seeks to define the situation in ways that produce insight. The emphasis is on producing a root definition which captures the essence of the problem situation in one or two sentences. Several root definitions may be produced to reflect different views if this is seen as fruitful. The root definition is created using a six-element checklist technique, CATWOE, described in "plain English" by Avison and Fitzgerald (1988, p. 247) as "*who* is doing *what* for *whom*, and to whom are they *answerable*, what *assumptions* are being made, and in what *environment* is it happening". In technical terms, however, the elements of the CATWOE acronym are:

> *C*ustomer or client is the 'whom', the beneficiary of the system.
> *A*ctor is 'who' carries out the change process.
> *T*ransformation is the 'what', the change taking place.
> *W*eltanschauung or world-view corresponds to the 'assumptions' made.
> *O*wner is the person 'answerable'.
> *E*nvironment is the 'environment' of the problem situation.

Stage 4: Model building

This stage is concerned with the logical expansion of the concise root definition into a conceptual model of the minimum necessary set of activities that must be done to achieve what is implied by the root definition. Wilson recommends that the model should contain fewer than 12 activities at the first level, due to human cognitive capacity constraints. These models are conceptual and can be structured using formal systems concepts or other systems thinking, such as the cybernetic model.

Stage 5: Comparison

This abstract conceptual model is compared with reality and differences identified. These differences are then resolved if possible through iterations of root definition and conceptual model stages.

Stages 6 and 7: Recommendations for change and taking action

The comparisons of stage 5 will have yielded a number of areas for changes that can be recommended as desirable. These changes must then be assessed to determine whether they are technically feasible and also whether they are culturally feasible for the relevant participants in the problem situation. When these feasibility issues have been satisfactorily resolved, the actions necessary to accomplish these changes are put in place.

Table 4.3 Stages of SSM

for SSM are suggested; firstly, Mode 1—"a formal stage-by-stage application of the method", and Mode 2—"an internal mental use of it as a thinking mode". The use of these modes in particular and the revised version of SSM in general have been critically evaluated by Jayaratna (1994).

Wilson points out that while SSM can be viewed as a linear, step by step, process, "it is more useful to regard it as a pattern of activities to be used in any order at any starting point". Also, in keeping with many of the soft approaches, it is something of a macro framework for development, in that it can complement other harder development approaches, perhaps by acting as a front-end for them as Avison and Fitzgerald (1988) have suggested.

Maybe the most important aspect of SSM is the impact it has had on the field of ISD, in the broadest sense. SSM has influenced numerous other approaches. SSM is still a rare example of a methodology based on a firm philosophical approach and on large empirical studies of the practice of ISD.

4.9   SOFTWARE PROCESS IMPROVEMENT AND THE CMM

In November 1986 the Software Engineering Institute (SEI) of Carnegie Mellon University in Pittsburgh, with assistance from the MITRE Corporation, began developing a process maturity framework to help organisations improve their software process. In June 1987 the SEI released a brief description of the software process maturity framework and in September they released the maturity questionnaire (Humphrey & Sweet, 1987). This assessment method was called the Process Maturity Model (PMM). Five years later, using knowledge acquired from software process assessments, software capability evaluations, and feedback from industry and government, the Capability Maturity Model (CMM) was proposed (Paulk, 1995).

The CMM is a five-layer model describing an evolutionary path from *ad hoc*, chaotic processes to mature, disciplined software processes. The five maturity levels describe successive foundations for continuous process improvement and define an ordinal scale for measuring the maturity of an organisation's software process. The advantage of the maturity levels is that they provide clear priorities, which provide guidance for selecting those few improvement activities that will be most helpful if implemented immediately.

The following are brief descriptions of the five maturity levels in the CMM framework and the primary process characteristics displayed at each level.

1.   **Initial**   The software process is characterised as *ad hoc*, and occasionally even chaotic. Few processes are defined, and success depends on individual effort and heroics. Until the process is under statistical control, orderly progress in process improvement is not possible.

2.   **Repeatable**   The organisation has achieved a stable process with a repeatable level of statistical control by initiating rigorous project management processes to track cost, schedule, and functionality. The necessary process discipline is in place to repeat earlier successes on projects with similar applications.

3.   **Defined**   The software process for both management and engineering activities is documented, standardised, and integrated into a standard software process for the organisation. All projects use an approved, tailored version of the organisation's standard software process for developing and maintaining software.

4.   **Managed**   Detailed measures of the software process and product quality are collected. Both the software process and products are quantitatively understood and controlled.

5.   **Optimising**   Continuous process improvement is enabled by quantitative feedback from the process and from piloting innovative ideas and technologies.

The staged structure of the CMM is based on principles of product quality using statistical control methods first promulgated in the 1930s by Walter Shewart, and further developed by W. Edwards Deming (Deming, 1986) and Joseph Juran (Juran, 1988; Juran, 1989). These principles were adapted by the SEI into a five-layer maturity framework, which was inspired by Philip Crosby's quality management maturity grid (Crosby, 1979).

The CMM is intended to be at a sufficient level of abstraction that it does not unduly constrain how the software process is implemented by an organisation; it simply describes what the essential attributes of a software process would normally be expected to be. Nor is the CMM prescriptive; it does not tell an organisation how to improve. The CMM describes an organisation at each maturity level without prescribing the specific means for getting there.

Each maturity level, with the exception of Level 1, is decomposed into constituent parts. This decomposition ranges from abstract summaries of each level down to their operational definition as key practices. Each maturity level is composed of several key process areas, which are further categorised into five sections called common features. The common features contain the key practices which collectively accomplish the goals of the key process area.

4.9.1   Stages of the CMM

Level 1 – The Initial Level

At the Initial Level, the organisation typically does not provide a stable environment for developing and maintaining software (Paulk *et al.*, 1993). The Initial process could properly be called ad hoc, and it is often even chaotic. Here, the organisation typically operates without formalised procedures, cost estimates and project plans. Tools are neither well integrated with the process nor uniformly applied. Change control is lax and there is little senior management exposure to or understanding of the problems and issues (Humphrey, 1988). During a crisis, projects typically abandon planned procedures and revert to coding and testing (Paulk *et al.*, 1993). Because many effective software actions such as design and code reviews or test data analysis do not appear to directly support shipping the product, they seem expendable. Since problems are often deferred or even forgotten, software installation and maintenance often present serious problems (Humphrey, 1988).

While organisations at this level may have formal procedures for project control, there is no management mechanism to ensure they are used. Success depends entirely on having an exceptional manager and a seasoned and effective software team; but when they leave the project their stabilising influence leaves with them. Even a strong engineering process cannot overcome the instability created by the absence of sound management practices (Paulk *et al.*, 1993). When an organisation lacks sound management practices, the benefits of good software engineering practices are undermined by ineffective planning and reaction-driven commitment systems.

The software process capability of Level 1 organisations is unpredictable because the software process is constantly changed or modified as the work progresses (Paulk *et al.*, 1993).

Level 2 – The Repeatable Level

At the Repeatable level, policies for managing a software project and procedures to implement those policies are established. Planning and managing new projects is based on experience with similar projects (Paulk *et al.*, 1993). One important strength of the Repeatable process over the Initial process is that it provides commitment control (Humphrey, 1988).

Organisations in Level 2 have installed basic software management controls. Realistic project commitments are based on the results observed on previous projects and on the requirements of the current project. The software managers for a project track software costs, schedules and functionality. Also, problems in meeting commitments are identified when they arise. Software requirements and the work products developed to satisfy them are base-lined, and their integrity is controlled. Software project standards are defined, and the organisation ensures they are faithfully followed. The software project team works with its sub-contractors, if any, to establish a strong customer-supplier relationship (Paulk *et al.*, 1993).

The software process capability of Level 2 organisations can be summarised as disciplined because planning and tracking of the software project is stable and earlier successes can be repeated. The project's process is under the effective control of a project management system.

Level 3 – The Defined Level

With the Defined Process, the organisation has achieved the foundation for major and continuing progress (Humphrey, 1988). The standard process for developing and maintaining software across the organisation is documented, including both software engineering and management processes, and these processes are integrated into a coherent whole. Project teams tailor this standard software process to develop their own defined software process. The project's defined software process contains an integrated set of well-defined software engineering and management processes. A well-defined process can be characterised as including readiness criteria, inputs, standards, and procedures for performing the work, verification mechanisms (such as peer reviews), outputs, and completion criteria. Because the software process is well defined, management has good insight into technical progress on all projects (Paulk *et al.*, 1993). The development group, when faced with a crisis, are likely to continue using the defined process (Humphrey, 1988).

The software process capability of Level 3 organisations can be summarised as standard and consistent because both software engineering and management activities are stable and repeatable. The process capability is based on a common, organisation-wide understanding of the activities, roles and responsibilities in a defined software process.

Level 4 – The Managed Level

At the Managed Level the organisation sets quantitative goals for both software products and processes. Productivity and quality are measured for software process activities across all projects as part of an organisational measurement initiative (Paulk *et al.*, 1993). The organisation establishes a process database to facilitate process quality and productivity analysis (Humphrey, 1988). These measurements establish the quantitative foundation for evaluating the projects' software processes and products.

Project teams achieve control over their products and processes by narrowing the variation in their process performance to fall within acceptable quantitative boundaries.

The software process capability of Level 4 organisations can be summarised as predictable because the process is measured and operates within measurable limits. This level of process capability allows an organisation to predict trends in process and product quality within the quantitative bounds of these limits. When these limits are exceeded, action is taken to correct the situation. Software products are of predictably high quality (Paulk *et al.*, 1993).

Level 5 – The Optimising Level

The move from the Managed to the Optimising Level represents a paradigm shift. Up to this point, software development managers have been largely product focused, and will typically only gather and analyse data that directly relates to product improvement. At the Optimising Level the data is available to actually tune the process itself (Humphrey, 1988). Data on the effectiveness of the software process is used to perform cost benefit analyses of new technologies and proposed changes to the organisation's software process. The organisation has the means to identify weaknesses and strengthen the process proactively, with the goal of preventing the occurrence of defects.

The software process capability of Level 5 organisations can be characterised as continuously improving the range of their process capability, thereby improving the process performance of their projects. Improvement occurs, both by incremental advancements in the existing process and by innovations using new technologies and methods.

4.9.2   Maturity Level Relationships

The CMM is a *descriptive* model in the sense that it describes essential attributes that would be expected to characterise an organisation at a particular maturity level (Paulk *et al.*, 1993). The CMM is not *prescriptive*; it does not tell an organisation how to improve. The CMM describes an organisation at each maturity level without prescribing the specific means for getting there. It can take several years to move from Level 1 to Level 2, for example, and moving between other levels will usually take a number of years also.

Success in Level 1 organisations depends on the (technical) competence and heroics of the people in the organisation. As projects grow in size and complexity, attention shifts from technical issues to organisational and managerial issues.

To achieve Level 2, management must focus on its own processes to achieve a disciplined software process before tackling technical and organisational issues at Level 3.

Level 3 builds on this project management foundation by defining, integrating, and documenting the entire software process. Integration in this case means that the outputs of one task flow smoothly into the inputs of the next task.

The focus of Level 4 is process control. The software process is managed so that it operates in a stable fashion within a zone of quality control, defined by upper and lower control limits. There may be spikes in the measured results, which breach these limits (referred to as *special causes*), but the system is generally stable overall. Because the process is both stable and measured, when some exceptional circumstance occurs, the "special cause" of the variation can be identified and addressed.

The focus of Level 5 is continuous process improvement. The software process is changed to improve quality, and the zone of quality control moves, in effect the upper and lower control limits are re-defined. There is random variation within the zone of quality control leading to re-work, and hence addressing *common causes* of variation comes to the fore.

Software process improvement initiatives such as the CMM have elicited an enormous level of interest among software development organisations and practitioners, although it has not been without some quite significant general criticism (Bollinger & McGowan, 1991; Bach, 1994), and even the question of its relevance to smaller software organisations has been investigated (Kautz, 1998). We return to this issue in Chapter 9 where method tailoring is discussed.

4.10   ENTERPRISE RESOURCE PLANNING (ERP) SYSTEMS

Enterprise Resource Planning (ERP) systems have been touted as the solution to many information systems problems such as incompatible systems and hardware platforms, the inability to integrate data throughout the business, inefficient business processes, and low productivity. ERP has as its goal the integration of an organisation's business processes across the entire supply chain—from supplier to customer. This integration of business systems promises many benefits, including streamlining business processes, data sharing, and potential cost savings. Other potential benefits include the removal of archaic systems and hardware which are expensive to maintain, and reductions in the number of personnel required. Major vendors of this type of software are SAP, Baan, PeopleSoft, JD Edwards, and Oracle. SAP has been recognised as the industry leader in terms of market share, followed by Oracle (Russo *et al.*, 1999).

ERP systems represent an attempt to achieve the single total information system for the organisation. However, this quest for the total system has several precedents in the IS field. Earlier attempts have been based on an assumption that it should be possible to treat the information within an organisation as one single resource, and that information technology is the way to make this resource available for use at all levels of the organisation. Over the years this assumption has been questioned. The basic issue of contention has been whether it is possible to implement a single information system or whether the complex organisational reality actually makes the idea impossible in practice. The arguments have changed over time. In the beginning the argument against the idea was, of course, that technology did not have necessary functionality and power to handle information in such a scale and of such complexity. Later arguments have been that the social complexity and the situatedness of an organisation make it impossible to use a system developed for generic use. Even if the discussion has been going back and forth, organisations have continuously tried to make the idea of the single total system become real.

In the late 1960s, for example, when it was realised that transaction processing systems were more data-oriented than information-oriented, and unsuited to the needs of management, a new category of information systems, namely management information systems, were proposed as a separate category of systems which would be the total system complementing transaction processing systems to satisfy all management's informational needs. Subsequently, an alternative approach emerged which sought to define all data and information concepts within an organisation. The idea was that when all these definitions were in place, it would be possible to use them in all systems and they would mean the same thing. The goal was to create a situation where information and data could flow between all parts and systems within the organisation.

However these first attempts to centralise organisational information systems were not very successful. Large organisations devoted enormous amounts of time and resources in a futile effort to reach what was considered the ultimate goal—a single information system for the entire organisation. The conclusion reached from these experiences was that it was impossible to define an all-encompassing information system from the 'bottom', i.e. based on the needs of the organisation.

One of the major, and almost never challenged assumptions of the time, was that information systems had to be developed to fit the activities and needs of the organisation. The idea that an organisation could adapt its activities to a predefined system was not regarded as a real option. The information system was seen as a 'tool', as something only supporting the organisation.

Over the years this basic assumption has been challenged. Maybe the first real challenge was realised in the notion of business process reengineering (BPR). The message of BPR was that an organisation had to break down its core activities to a low level of detail. When the analysis and breakdown was accomplished, they should be rebuilt, but now based on the opportunities created by technology. This meant that the activities had to be reengineered to fit the technology, instead of the reverse. This was a clear break with the dominating tradition. Even though BPR was not successful on a larger scale, the concept paved the way for a reversed view of information systems development, that is, to adapt the organisation to an already existing system. ERP systems build on this new assumption, which suggests it is possible to develop one total socio-technical system by starting with an already existing information system and adapting the organisation to that system.

The ERP phenomenon has in many ways changed the preconditions for systems development, for the use of methods, and for the developers themselves.

4.11   OPEN SOURCE SOFTWARE

A full discussion of the open source software phenomenon is beyond the scope of this book, but a detailed treatment of the topic can be found in Feller & Fitzgerald (2002). Briefly summarising, open source software is software in which the distribution should include the source code (or it should be downloadable at no cost), the code should be modifiable, and the code should be re-distributable without conditions by third-parties. Commercial software on the other hand has traditionally been sold for a fee, with considerable restrictions on use, is distributed only in binary executable (closed source) form, and may not be modified or re-distributed except by vendor. Open source software should not be confused with freeware or shareware, however, as it is distributed under a very detailed licence which guarantees its continuing openness. A brief history of open source software is provided next by way of background.

In the early days of computing, software was shared freely. In fact, it was considered something of an achievement to get programs to run at all, thus, if software worked it was shared widely. A significant event in the early days was the 1950s US government consent decree which prevented the telecommunications giant, AT&T, from entering other commercial markets (Leonard, 2000). This effectively ensured that the AT&T-developed Unix operating system would have to be distributed free of charge. One of the most effective and well-known distribution channels for Unix and related software was the Berkeley Software Distribution (BSD), established in 1977 at the University of Berkeley in California. Another major milestone in the free software arena was the establishment of the Free Software Foundation (FSF) by Richard Stallman in 1985. Prophetically, Stallman foresaw a scenario whereby a monopoly could arise through the closed software model. Stallman devoted his attention to creating a suite of free software products, the GNU family (GNU being a recursive acronym that stands for GNU's Not Unix). The strong ideological nature of the FSF is evident from the terms of the licence policy associated with it, the general public license (GPL), which dictated that if a software distribution contained any FSF software, then all the software in the distribution had also to be covered by the GPL—termed a viral licence for that reason.

In 1991, the most high profile OSS product, the Linux operating system, was begun by a 21-year-old Helsinki university student, Linus Torvalds, who adapted the Minix (a derivative of Unix) system to create a Unix-like operating system for the IBM PC. With a commendable degree of modesty, Torvalds openly sought help on the project, and succeeded in attracting a great deal of support worldwide. Estimates suggest that more than a thousand developers have collaborated on the Linux kernel development alone. By any standards, Linux is a phenomenal success; indeed, it is assumed by many to be synonymous with the OSS approach. From these humble beginnings, within ten years, Linux had grown to hold 25 per cent of the general server market and 34 per cent of the Internet/Web server market. A survey carried out by the IDC group predicts that its market-share will grow faster than all other operating systems combined through 2003.

Another notable OSS product is the Apache web-server, begun in February 1995 by a group of web software developers who decided to pool their expertise rather than duplicate work by reinventing the wheel in isolation. As of April 2001, Apache had achieved an astonishing 63 per cent of the web-server market (Netcraft survey, 2001).

Although Linux and Apache are high profile, the more significant success of OSS can be seen behind the scenes, in the Internet 'category killers' such as BIND, which runs the Domain Name Server (DNS) for the World Wide Web, and reckoned to be the most mission-critical Internet application; Sendmail, which is central to the Internet mail backbone, and which is estimated to be the mail agent for 80 per cent of Internet mail.

In February 1998, a group sympathetic to some of the ideals of the free software movement, but conscious of the interpretation of 'free' to mean 'no cost' or *gratis*, and also of the zealous, anti-commercial perception of the free software movement among the business community, coined the 'open source' term, and established a license which was less restrictive than the GPL. Basically, the open source licence required that any open source software distribution would include the source code (or make it downloadable at no cost) and that the code would be modifiable (indeed, modifications would be desirable and encouraged), and that the code would be re-distributable without conditions by third-parties.

Linus Torvalds was an early supporter of the group—a very significant imprimatur. Richard Stallman of the Free Software Foundation was not—also significant. One of the critical enablers of the growth of the OSS movement arose from Netscape's decision to release the source code of their Navigator web browser. Netscape had dropped to 13 per cent of market-share, and were facing a crisis which threatened their survival, as they faced such extreme competition from Microsoft's Internet Explorer browser. They decided to take the radical step of releasing the source code of their browser as a survival strategy—the Mozilla[2] project as it was called. While the Mozilla project has not been an unqualified success (Lewis, 1999; Williams, 2000), it is certainly the case that the Mozilla project made the corporate world take notice of OSS.

The open source movement has attracted a huge amount of media, commercial and academic interest. The media are probably attracted by the David v. Goliath fairy-tale aspects of the phenomenon, whereby the might of commercial software giants like Microsoft can be challenged by the efforts of an army of globally-located idealistic volunteers. Commercial interest was certainly stimulated by the Netscape Mozilla project, but also, IBM, Corel, Intel, Ericsson and HP, to name but a few, quickly announced various degrees of support for the OSS initiative.

---

[2] Mozilla is alleged to have been the internal name for the initial Netscape browser project, labelled '*Mozilla, the Mosaic Killer*,' thus reflecting the mission at the time of eliminating the competition from the Mosaic browser. It is somewhat ironic that Netscape chose the name when they in turn were facing potentially fatal competition from Microsoft's Internet Explorer browser.

4.12   CHAPTER SUMMARY

In this chapter we examined some of the more non-traditional approaches to systems development, including RAD and XP. These methods seek to address some of the problems identified with traditional ISD, including projects that are late, over-budget and deliver systems that do not meet the needs of users. By shortening the development life cycle, not only is the cost of development reduced, but also the system is more likely to address the dynamic nature of the environment. User participation and iterative identification of system requirements result in systems that are more closely aligned with the needs of the users. By addressing the social and organisational aspects of information systems, otherwise unforeseen problems such as lack of fit with the organisation's culture can be avoided and issues such as workers' rights can be taken into account.

The next section of the chapter addressed a means of evaluating or measuring the quality of the systems development process. The Capability Maturity Model describes characteristics of development organisations at various levels of maturity, where a high level of maturity implies a better (more controlled, repeatable, measurable) process. Organisations can use this model to access their level of maturity and to determine what changes are needed to move to higher levels. The CMM influences the method-in-action when an organisation changes the way a method is implemented in order to meet the objectives of a targeted maturity level. The final sections of the chapter addressed some of the more recent phenomena which have major implications for IS development, ERP systems which represent perhaps the extreme use of a software package approach, and open source software which seems to subvert the traditional wisdom of IS development. These latter phenomena are discussed in more detail in Chapter 10.

This chapter has focused on the 'radical' approaches. However, it is worth bearing in mind, and it is a point reinforced by the historical perspective of the last two chapters, that many of the so-called radical and innovative methods have very strongly grounded historical predecessors. For example, the chief programmer team (Baker, 1972; Mills, 1971) and 'egoless programming' concepts (Weinberg, 1971) have clear parallels in those methods or development approaches which have emerged more recently. Thus, the extent to which these new approaches can live up to their billing as a 'silver bullet' is very arguable. Many of the fundamental principles underpinning these methods have actually been quite well established for some time, and are thus not very innovative in that respect. However, the actual merit and usefulness of what are the new and innovative principles proposed in these methods has yet to be proven. Indeed, in relation to some of these newer methods, we are tempted to suggest Mark Twain's memorable judgement: 'they are both original and true; unfortunately, the bits that are true are not original, and the bits that are original are not true'.

4.13   DISCUSSION QUESTIONS

1.   The soft systems methodology (SSM) explicitly acknowledges the mindset of the developer as a relevant component of the ISD context. Discuss ways in which the developer's mindset can influence the ISD process.

2.   Many of the recent innovations in ISD could be accused of being 'old wine in new bottles' in that they are primarily just repackaging concepts that have emerged in an earlier era. Try to identify some instances of this, based on the historical evidence provided in the last two chapters.

3.   The Rational Unified Process appears to follow the phases of the systems development life cycle, yet it is not viewed by the authors as a traditional SDLC approach. How is RUP different from most approaches that follow the SDLC?

4.   The phenomenon of Enterprise Resource Planning (ERP) systems has undoubtedly had an impact on the development of information systems. Would you consider ERP to be a system development method? Why or why not?

5.   What impacts—positive or negative—could the Capability Maturity Model (CMM) have on the information systems development process and on the resulting systems?

5

From Formalised Method to Method-in-Action: The Rational and Political Roles of Methods

5.1 INTRODUCTION

The previous two chapters have provided some background on ISD methods. In this chapter we deal with the relationship between formalised methods and method-in-action, and how this is mediated by the roles that methods play (see Fig. 5.1). The chapter identifies a set of *rational roles* of method which are used to justify formalised methods, as these roles form the conceptual basis underpinning the use of formalised methods. There are also a number of pressures which currently support increased formalisation of the development process, including a bias in the ISD literature which depicts developer practices as irrational, and which strongly favours the adoption of formalised ISD methods. As a counterpoint, however, the chapter also identifies some factors and pressures which question the value of formalised methods. A set of *covert political roles* which methods can play are also presented. These serve to influence the derivation of the method-in-action.

5.2 FACTORS THAT SUPPORT THE USE OF FORMALISED METHODS

Early efforts at systems development often relied on unsystematic and random methods, although some systematic approaches to systems development were actually available (as discussed in Chapter 3). By the end of the 1960s, the systems development problems, which gave rise to the term, 'software crisis', were widely

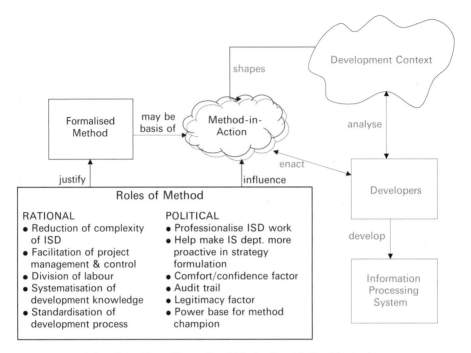

Fig. 5.1   From Formalised Method to Method-in-Action

acknowledged. As already stated, the software crisis referred to the fact that systems took too long to develop, cost too much, and did not work very well. Furthermore, since the systems which needed to be developed were becoming increasingly complex, the situation would inevitably be further exacerbated. Thus, a more disciplined approach to ISD was advocated—in general culminating in a belief in the use of formalised methods.

Some of the fundamental concepts underpinning the general rationale for development methods are discussed in subsequent sections. These factors form a set of rational or intellectual roles that methods may overtly play in ISD, and are summarised in Fig. 5.1. They are countered by a set of political roles that are more covert in nature—again these are summarised in Fig. 5.1, and are discussed later in Section 5.4.

The arguments presented below in favour of methods have a long history and are not indisputable. In this presentation we have chosen to describe them in the form they have been used by their promoters. Therefore it is important to remember that these arguments are not necessarily universally accepted as true within the field of IS, but they constitute an important part of the historical—and present—rationale behind the use of formalised methods in ISD.

5.2.1   Reductionist Subdivision of Complex Development Process

At heart, formalised ISD methods involve a strategy which implies a subdivision of the development process. The 'divide and conquer' principle has long been a feature of mathematical and engineering approaches to problem solving, and the early development methods were very much influenced by technical and engineering disciplines. Thus, a reductionist approach was taken through which the overall development process is differentiated into a series of individual stages. Floyd (1987, p. 199) captured this philosophy well as based on the

> *need to take reductionist steps with respect to the richness of reality in order to specify a microworld suitable for modelling in a computer system.*

An influential early contribution was that of Börje Langefors (1973) who, in arguing for a more formal approach to system development, outlined the foundations for a theory of information systems. He conceptualised systems development as a rational and scientific process, and proposed a subdivision of the development process into deciding *what* an information system must do, and *how* it should do it.

Langefors adopted a mechanistic view of organisations with optimal satisfaction of organisational goals as a central component, and such a view is evident in many current development methods. Based on a rational scientific view, prevalent in many other disciplines, the development process is broken into the broad categories of analysis of requirements, design of a solution, and implementation of that solution. Other broad categories to be added include an initial investigation of the organisational problem context, and a final maintenance stage. Thus, systems development is conceptualised as a linear model, relying on phases ordered in time and leading to increasingly formal defining documents until the system eventually emerges. This leads to the key concept of a system development life-cycle (SDLC), discussed in Chapter 3, which contains as a central premise the subdivision of system development into several distinguishable sequential phases, and which may be traced to the scientific reductionist mode of enquiry prevalent at the time.

5.2.2   Facilitation of Project Management and Control

The phased approach to systems development has many implications. One of the widely-cited benefits is that it makes the development process more amenable to project management and control. Visibility into the development process is improved and at the end of each phase there is an opportunity to review progress, monitor actual costs and benefits and compare with expected figures. This helps to minimise the risk inherent in systems development projects. Methods also facilitate a control dimension by providing a coherent framework within which steering committees, walkthrough techniques, audit procedures, quality control and inspection practices can be incorporated. Development methods also afford a structural framework for the development process in providing a taxonomy of the necessary component activities of development. Redundant, irrational and counter-productive activities can therefore be eliminated. Additionally, the grouping of activities improves efficiency by ensuring that necessary work is completed without oversight.

5.2.3   Economies Afforded by the Division of Labour

Another implication, which arises from the reduction of the development process into a series of individual phases, is that a division of labour is possible. Since each phase is comprised of different tasks requiring different skills—for example, analysis, programming, and technical writing—some economies of specialisation are afforded. For example, not every labour category participates in every development stage. The finer granularity achieved through the subdivision of the labour process allows organisations to use differential pay rates depending on the particular skills required, rather than having to pay for all-round ability in every phase of development.

5.2.4   Systematisation of Development Knowledge

Closely related to the division of labour rationale is the notion of gathering and systematising knowledge. Both are fundamental principles of Taylor's scientific management which sought to find the 'one best way' to perform work. The objective is to change all subject-dependent knowledge into knowledge in an objective form. The idea being that knowledge separated from a specific subject is valued more because it makes knowledge into something possible to handle and manipulate. The transfer of knowledge from the designer to the method also leads to a lesser dependency on specific persons, and that is seen as desirable by some method advocates (see Chapter 7). This formalisation of knowledge in the ISD method allows it to be stored, systematised, disseminated and exchanged. It facilitates the transfer of knowledge from skilled and knowledgeable developers to those less skilled, thus shortening the learning curve for the latter.

5.2.5   Standardisation of the Development Process

One of the implications of this formalisation of knowledge is that it affords a standardisation of the development process. This facilitates inter-changeability among developers—particularly important given that developers have traditionally shown more loyalty to their profession than to individual companies. Following a standardised process may improve co-ordination and communication among the many participants in complex development projects, and it may also ease subsequent maintenance problems. As already mentioned above, development methods specify a structure for the development process, and this may help to promote discipline among developers. Also, a standardised development process can lead to increased productivity, in that specific resources may be provided in a 'just in time' fashion to ensure that systems are built faster. Another potential benefit is that of increased quality which follows from the issues discussed above, and also from the fact that systems can be designed according to a standardised process which incorporates flexibility and adequate documentation.

5.3   PRESSURES FOR INCREASED FORMALISM IN THE DEVELOPMENT PROCESS

In addition to the aforementioned arguments supporting the use of methods, there are a number of influential sources which are causing an increased pressure in favour of the use of formalised development methods (summarised in Table 5.1). For example, at a broad level the ISO-certification process, much sought after by organisations, requires the use of formalised development processes. Also, major institutions such as the UK government have mandated the use of the SSADM method (see Chapter 3) for systems development. SSADM is now used on projects totalling billions of pounds each year, and this causes a significant pressure in the industry to move in this direction—a fact which is borne out in the large numbers of organisations supplying consultancy, training, and CASE tools supporting the SSADM method. Several other national governments have also adopted SSADM as the required development method, while countries such as France, Holland, and Italy have their own formalised development methods.

- Desirability of ISO-certification
- Government development standards:
    SSADM (UK, Ireland, Malta, Hong Kong, Israel)
    Dafne (Italy)
    Merise (France)
    NIAM (Netherlands)
    Department of Defense Std. 2167 (US)
- Capability Maturity Model (CMM) programme from Software Engineering Institute
- ISD literature bias in favour of formalised methods:
    Irrational practitioners assumed to be reason for problems in systems
        development
    Formalised methods seen as solution to development problems

Table 5.1   Pressures for Increased Formalism of ISD

Similarly in the US, the Department of Defense (DoD) have established development standards (e.g. DoD Std. 2167) for software development which developers working on DoD projects must follow. These standards have emerged from several years of research and are intended to allow the DoD more visibility and control with respect to the development process. Also, the DoD has recently collaborated with the Software Engineering Institute on the Capability Maturity Model (see Chapter 4). This programme is concerned with assessing the capability of organisations to produce quality software in a timely and repeatable fashion and it has generated intense focus in the US software industry. However, this programme places great emphasis on adherence to formalised development procedures.

5.3.1   ISD Literature Bias in Favour of Formalised Methods

Although not actually borne out in empirical studies, the general implication in much of the ISD literature is that practitioners are moving, albeit very slowly, towards more widespread adoption of formalised methods, and that this should help to alleviate the problems inherent in systems development. The following quotes represent some of the prevalent thinking on this issue. These quotes are divided into two sets. The first set depicts the poor regard in which practitioners are generally held by ISD researchers, the manner of their practice being viewed as the real source of problems. The second set shows how the formalisation of practice by adherence to ISD methods is seen by many researchers as an appropriate step towards a solution:

Irrational Practice

> *The average coder ... (is) ... generally introverted, sloppy, inflexible, in over his head, and undermanaged.*
>
> (Boehm, 1976)

> *The majority of software development organisations operate in a 'Realm of Darkness', blissfully unaware of even the rudimentary concepts of structured analysis and design.*
>
> (Yourdon, 1991)

> *... the lack of professional discipline among the great unwashed masses of systems developers.*
>
> (Ward, 1992a)

Methods as Appropriate Step Towards Solution

The next set of quotes illustrate the prevalence of the view that increased adoption of methods represents an appropriate step towards solving the problems associated with software development:

The major forces working for diversity appear to be ignorance, lassitude, deficiency . . . Employers have been very relaxed about setting and enforcing local standards for their employees to follow.

(Chapin, 1980)

The problems faced in developing large software include . . . enforcing a method on the developers.

(Ramamoorthy et al., 1984)

The first effect of teaching a method—rather than disseminating knowledge—is that of enhancing the capacities of the already capable, thus magnifying the difference in intelligence.

(Dijkstra, 1972)

Losers consist of unnamed, unspecified, up to the individual, or 'written-but not formalised' types of methods.

(Zolnowski & Ting, 1982)

Structured design is an enormous step forward from the traditional, seat of the pants, methods.

(King, 1984)

The use of a formalised SDM is perceived as positive and well advised.

(Jenkins et al., 1984)

Software development in professional communities often is completely ad hoc, or at best supported by structured methods . . . and JSD.

(Plat et al., 1991)

Progressive companies and a few insightful government agencies recognised the advantages of (3rd generation SDMs) . . . many were not able to assimilate such a high level of sophistication.

(Couger et al., 1982)

One startling and somewhat disturbing observation is that many (systems development) methods are used very little.

(Palvia & Nosek, 1993)

These are just a small sample, which illustrate the widespread bias in the literature. However, one of the effects of this bias has been the search for the method equivalent of the holy grail—the method which represents the 'best way' to develop systems. This has led to a trend whereby competing methods have been developed, a phenomenon discussed in relation to the structured approach in Chapter 3, and well expressed by Tagg (1983) who draws a parallel with the proliferation of religious sects:

Despite the fact that they are 95% agreed in their aims and their broad areas of getting there, they nevertheless manage to stay separate. Each sect jealously guards its own style and magic ingredients.

However, this literature bias is especially problematic when one considers the circular pressure this creates, in that even though the literature may not *reflect* actual practice, it certainly *influences* it, thus creating a significant additional pressure in support of the use of formalised methods.

5.4   FACTORS THAT MILITATE AGAINST THE USE OF FORMALISED METHODS

The assumption that formalised development methods actually represent the most appropriate means of solving the software crisis is open to question. This section presents a number of critical arguments which serve to question the extent to which formalised methods contribute usefully to the development process. These factors are summarised in Table 5.2, and are discussed in subsequent sections.

Definitional Anomalies:
Problems as to what exactly constitutes a method

Fundamental differences between some methods and artificial, contrived differences between others

Generalisation Without Adequate Conceptual and Empirical Foundation:
Absence of independent peer review and verification in non-trivial situation

Inadequacies of Rational Scientific Paradigm:
Systems development is not actually an orderly rational process but most methods view it as such

Over-emphasis on technical rationality at the expense of softer, social aspects

Goal Displacement:
Slavish and blind adherence to method while losing sight of the fact that development of an actual system is the real objective

Assumption that Methods are Universally Applicable:
Failure to recognise contingency factors and the uniqueness of every development situation

Inadequate Recognition of Developer-Embodied Factors:
Methods do not cater for factors critical to successful development, such as individual creativity and intuition, or learning over time

---

Table 5.2   Factors that Militate Against the Use of Methods

5.4.1   Definitional Anomalies

When it comes to deciding what actually constitutes a development method, the definitional quagmire so common in the computing field becomes apparent. Methods have been variously defined in terms of models, management practices, technical practices, tools, training procedures and so on. Also, despite the large number of methods available, it has been suggested that there may not be significant differences between different methods. The contrived and artificial differentiation between the structured approach and its competitors was discussed in Chapter 3. Indeed, it has even been argued that the 'software crisis' is an exaggeration, that software is the success story of our time (Glass 1998), and that the reason for this exaggeration has been to rationalise new development approaches in the software development arena (DeGrace & Stahl, 1990).

However, there are also fundamental differences between some methods in terms of philosophy, objective and techniques. Methods may differ radically in paradigm—from 'hard' technically-oriented to 'soft' human-oriented (as discussed in Chapters 3 and 4), and in focus, as some methods do not cover phases such as systems planning or requirements analysis while others do not cover system implementation.

5.4.2   Generalisation without Adequate Validation

Methods have frequently been constructed by abstracting practices and techniques from successful development projects, and formalising these into a set of guidelines and procedures to form a development method, but there may be little philosophical justification. Lyytinen (1987) identified an inadequate conceptual base as a weakness in many methods, pointing out that most have "an ambiguous and narrow conception of the phenomena IS developers confront", with few methods providing definitions of basic terms. Lyytinen further argued that methods have very limited theoretical foundations and thus have difficulty in dealing with "the hazards of social change introduced by the systems design".

There is a general process which should be followed before a method may be recommended for professional use. Firstly, there needs to be a sound conceptual foundation. Generally, this is achieved in the physical and social sciences through a peer review process in which experts in the field, who have no vested interest in the method or technique, examine it for theoretical shortcomings. The second strand of the process is to obtain empirical evidence of usability, which requires the method or technique to have been successfully applied to a non-trivial problem situation. However, there is little evidence that the formalised methods currently available have ever been subject to these basic criteria. Certainly, the structured approach, the "most popular systems development method in North America and Europe"

(Yourdon, 1991), seems not to have been subject to such criteria, but was based on the intuition of its founders that it would work rather than on any real-world experience (Ward, 1992a).

5.4.3   Inadequacies of the Rational Scientific Paradigm

The underlying paradigm for many development methods is the scientific reductionist one. They rest on the *a priori* assumptions that the solution can be arrived at through a series of technically-devised steps, and that the developer can obtain detailed knowledge about the problem situation. These assumptions are critically examined here.

The conceptualisation of development as following a linear sequence of phases is implicit in the systems development life-cycle (SDLC). The problems of the SDLC have been discussed in some detail already in Chapter 4 where prototyping approaches were introduced. Summarising very briefly, the principal weakness of the SDLC is that later phases depend on the successful completion of earlier phases. However, later phases are much more likely to take place in the context of incomplete earlier phases.

Systems development in practice is not an orderly systematic phased process. Developers do not develop systems by completing a single task and moving on to the next task following a rational sequence; rather they will have a range of tasks not concluded due to the interdependent nature of development. Requirements specification and systems design are heavily interdependent, but in the phased approach to development the *what* of requirements specification is strictly separated from the *how* of design. This is extremely problematic. As Peters (1981) put it: "one cannot state a problem without some rudimentary notion of what the solution should be".

This view of the systems development process as an intertwined, all-at-once process has been also borne out in our empirical research, as methods were modified in all the organisations in which they were in use. Also, it was recognised that the development approach often differed from that prescribed by the method, but that the work was later 'retrofitted' to comply with method requirements, thus creating the illusion that the method-prescribed sequence was followed.

As is evident from the sample of quotes from the ISD literature in Section 5.3.1 above, one of the main assumptions underpinning the belief in development methods is that practitioners are perceived as biased towards following irrational design practices, and thus require the support of a method which provides a rational basis for development. However, methods tend to conform to a very particular technical rationality in which, to use Schon's (1987) terms:

Rigorous professional practitioners solve well-formed instrumental problems by applying theory and technique derived from systematic, preferably scientific knowledge.

Much research has questioned the validity of viewing systems development as a rational process. For example, Robey & Markus (1984) showed that while the various phases of systems development can be explained by rational motives, they could also be explained as political rituals which are used to negotiate the private interests of the various parties concerned. Thus, the stages in systems development can be explained by two diametrically-opposed sets of motives—rational and political. However, as discussed above, the rational motives are the ones assumed in many methods, and consequently, they do not cope well with social and human factors. System development is not just a technical process; social influences and consequences need to be considered also. Yet, as discussed in Chapter 4, many development methods only pay lip-service to social aspects.

Parnas & Clements (1986) also argued that the rational approach to systems development which is part of many development methods is not valid, as it is a much less tidy process in practice. However, there are good reasons for performing some purification or sanitisation on the results of systems development to "fake" a rational approach to development. Anyone who must work on the system after it is developed will "want to understand the programs, not relive their discovery", and this is best achieved by access to the polished output of what can justifiably masquerade as having been a rational process. Indeed, Parnas & Clements (p. 256) concluded:

> It is very hard to be a rational designer; even faking that process is quite difficult. However, the result is a product that can be understood, maintained, and reused.

5.4.4   Goal Displacement

The goal displacement phenomenon basically refers to the situation whereby developers become preoccupied with adherence to the method at the expense of actual development; that is, the developer becomes engrossed in following the method and loses sight of the fact that development of a system is the real goal. Further compounding the problem is the fact that many methods include logically-redundant tasks so as to improve reliability, but developers may often perform unnecessary tasks and omit necessary ones.

Ironically, even in the Garmisch conference of 1968 where the term 'software crisis' was coined, and the need for more rigorous development procedures strongly voiced, some participants warned of the potential dangers of the rigid application of methods. Smith (quoted in Naur *et al.*, 1976, p. 88) described his experience with the rigid adherence to methods in his organisation:

> They begin with planning specifications, go through functional specifications, implementation specifications, etc. This activity is represented by a PERT chart with many nodes. If you look down the PERT chart you discover that all the nodes on it up until

the last one produce nothing but paper. It is unfortunately true that in my organisation people confuse the menu with the meal.

De Grace & Stahl (1990) reinforce this point. Their analysis of the development documentation from several projects found more than 90 per cent of the content was devoted to reporting about the status of the development process, while less than 10 per cent described what was to be done or how to do it.

The goal displacement phenomenon was identified as a major problem in our empirical research, with one developer referring to the requirement of their method to produce entity life histories to illustrate this problem:

Drawing entity life history models can be an industry in itself, and, in the end, it may only serve to clarify the obvious.

The clear moral is that when it takes so much effort to comply with method requirements, it may be more worthwhile to spend the time on actual development. There is a need therefore to distinguish between form and substance when following a method.

5.4.5   Assumption that Methods are Universally Applicable

There is a tendency in Western society to view certain procedures as universally applicable. Relating this to ISD methods, it manifests itself in the belief that methods are appropriate for all development situations, the "one size fits all" presumption as Chikofsky (1989) has labelled it. However, as discussed in Chapters 3 and 4, this does not accord due consideration to the contingencies of each development situation. DeMarco, one of the pioneering figures of the structured approach, was forthright in his criticism of such a strategy (1982, p. 13):

I find myself more and more exasperated with the great inflexible sets of rules that many companies pour into concrete and sanctify as methods ... Use the prevailing method only as a starting point for tailoring.

In practice, developers frequently do not apply the methods in their complete form as specified. Developers omit those aspects of the method that do not seem to suit the contingencies of the situation. For example, the US Department of Defense, whose strong advocacy of formalised methods has already been discussed, recommends tailoring of their recommended standard method, DoD Std. 2167, to suit the particular development situation. Similarly, Motorola, one of the leading software development organisations in the world, have a very sophisticated method tailoring strategy to create their method-in-action (cf. Fitzgerald *et al.*, 2002). This tailoring strategy is discussed in more detail in Chapter 9.

As discussed above, part of the rationale behind the use of development methods is to facilitate project management and control of the development process. Indeed, methods have an intuitive appeal for management by seeming to introduce rigour into the development process. However, Glass (1991) has rejected this as illusory, comparing the use of a development method to the effect of the Maginot line—giving the "illusion of quality but hiding violations". Development methods attempt to impose complete solutions when the minimum are not yet well-defined. Glass suggests that the software field is too young for "premature positions and posturings". He argues that methods focus on the trappings of design rather than on its essence which is actually the cognitive activity in the mind of the developer. This issue is discussed further in Chapter 7 where developer factors are considered.

The tendency to view methods as universally applicable is a very serious one. The method is accorded a central role and the overt rational roles of the method are perceived as paramount, with the contribution of the developer played down. This is particularly problematic as it fails to recognise the importance of learning over time as developers increase their expertise. Another problem arises in that strict adherence to the method may impose a considerable inertia on the development process as the individual steps are scrupulously followed, thus resulting in a very cumbersome development process. Methods are perhaps best viewed as an organising framework, and it is vital that they be tailored to the actual development situation. Certainly, developers should not follow methods blindly, dogmatically plodding through idealised checklists. Rather, it is vital that a method-in-action be configured, uniquely tailored to the needs of the development context, and taking advantage of the developer abilities.

5.4.6   Inadequate Recognition of Developer-Embodied Factors

This factor will be discussed in detail in Chapter 7, and so it is just briefly summarised here. The ingenuity and ability of the developer cannot be compounded into any development method. However, the varied skill levels of different developers is not acknowledged in formalised methods. IS development is a creative process, and blind, slavish adherence to a method may actually preclude innovation. The importance of individual differences in systems development has been widely reported, with estimates that developer factors have more than six times greater effect on development productivity than the use of software tools (Boehm, 1981). Nor do methods allow for the learning experience and greater problem domain knowledge that developers gain over time. Each systems development project is generally undertaken as if it was unique. Yet, in a comparative study of successful and unsuccessful systems analysts, Vitalari & Dickson (1983) emphasised the importance of learning over time. They concluded that developers acquired a "repertoire of strategies" to apply in different system development situations.

Pressures for New Approaches to ISD:
Changing Nature of Business Environment
Short-term needs dominate given 'faster metabolism' of business today

Altered Profile of ISD Environment
Configuration development: integration of package software to incorporate local practices

Replacement of large-scale monolithic approaches with approaches based on a 'good enough' and 'frequent tangible results' philosophy

Table 5.3 Pressures for New Approaches to ISD

5.5 PRESSURES FOR NEW APPROACHES TO ISD

In addition to these problematic issues discussed above, there are a number of pressures for new and radical approaches to systems development which also question the use of formalised development methods. These issues have to do with the changing nature of the business environment in general, the changing profile of the systems development environment in particular, and the need for more rapid delivery of systems to meet short-term needs. These issues are summarised in Table 5.3 and are discussed in the following section. They will also be discussed in Chapter 6 which considers the development context.

5.5.1 Changing Nature of Business Environment

The accelerating pace of change characteristic of the business environment facing organisations today is a common theme in contemporary research. This acceleration requires organisations to act more effectively in shorter time-frames. However, formalised methods are oriented towards large-scale development with a long development time, but the continuous change that organisations are now faced with, means that short-term needs dominate, and these in turn mean that the economics of formalised systems development is dwindling. Developers, thus, do not have the luxury of being able to patiently follow a comprehensive method. Indeed, the truncation of some phases in the development process is probably inevitable.

5.5.2 Changing Profile of Systems Development Environment

There has been a major change in software development in the past few years, with companies relying far less on in-house development of systems, but pursuing alternative strategies such as buying package software, ERP systems being an extreme case of this (see Chapter 4), or outsourcing system development. In this context, information systems are constructed on the basis of several suppliers' modules, integrated together by specially written software which incorporates local practice. This altered development profile further serves to question the economics of formalised development as current formalised methods do not address such a mode of development. Also, as discussed earlier, organisations cannot afford to wait several months or years for systems to be developed, and are seeking an accelerated development approach. Indeed, as mentioned earlier, researchers have estimated a need for a tenfold increase in system development productivity (Verity, 1987). Hough (1993) also called for a change in philosophy from large-scale monolithic approaches:

> In the past, this philosophy has framed application development as a process that follows a long, unbending path, resulting in software that is anything but soft. Many applications are developed using a monolithic approach even though business needs and requirements change over time.

Hough cited evidence from an IBM study which discussed the problems that can arise from monolithic development approaches. These include a slowed pace of development; treatment of the project as a "career"; lost sight of the original business problem; loss of interest by the development staff; deterioration of morale among individuals participating in the project. Hough proposes a rapid delivery approach to development as a solution to these problems. The main thrust of rapid delivery is to produce frequent tangible results, that is, every few months some functional capability is delivered (see discussion of RAD in Chapter 4).

5.6   RATIONAL AND POLITICAL ROLES OF METHOD

Two broad, but diametrically opposed, categories of roles that methods can play in the development process have been identified in the framework in Fig. 5.1, namely a set of rational roles and a set of political roles. These are discussed in turn here.

5.6.1   Rational Roles of Methods

The rational roles played by methods are a set of overt, intellectual ones, and are represented by the factors which form part of the conceptual basis and arguments behind the use of methods as discussed in Section 5.2 above. As can be seen from that discussion, these roles are quite well documented in the literature. Our empirical research into ISD has also confirmed the importance of these factors.

The project management role was emphasised in all the organisations studied. The typical view was expressed by the IS manager in a government department who stated that it made for "more effective management of the systems development process". Likewise, in a food processing co-operative, an interviewee stressed the increased transparency into the development process that methods provide. He identified the importance of the explicit identification of milestones which have to be achieved during development, thus allowing for a "more planned duration" of development projects. A similar view was echoed by the IS manager in one software house who stressed the importance of "curbing the optimism of developers who answered too quickly in the affirmative" when pressed by clients on the schedule for systems delivery. By making explicit all the steps that comprise the development process, developers were made more aware of the size and complexity of the task.

This latter issue is related to the communication role that methods provide. The IS manager in a government department referred to the "communication layer" that their method provided. Also, another interviewee referred to the manner in which the method forced a level of abstraction of the development process, thus "forcing one to stand back and not jump straight in to development." Again, interviewees in several organisations stressed the importance of providing a template for inexperienced developers (this issue is discussed in more detail in Chapter 7 which focuses on developer factors). In a similar vein, the project leader in a public utility company mentioned the need for methods to play a role in helping to learn from previous development project experiences.

5.6.2   Political Roles of Methods

A set of political roles that methods may play have also been identified in our research. These are diametrically opposed to the rational overt ones and are more covert in nature. Most have not been identified previously in the ISD literature. Summarising briefly, they include the following:

- Contribution to 'professionalising' ISD work, thus insulating developers from conceding to unreasonable deadlines and demands from user departments.
- Help in promotion of IS department to a more proactive role in strategy formulation.
- Comfort or confidence factor, whereby method use provides some reassurance that 'proper' practices are being followed, or provides confidence that development decisions have been made on a systematic basis.
- Audit trail of the development process to afford protection if design decisions turn out to be wrong in the future.
- Legitimacy factor, whereby organisations claim to use a method to win contracts with government agencies, or to help achieve ISO-certification.
- Provision of a 'power-base' for method champions who may use it to raise their profile within an organisation.

In our empirical research, interviewees readily identified the political roles that methods can play. For example, the project manager in the food processing company identified the role of the method in contributing to "professionalising" the work of the IS department. He suggested that "it draws a seriousness to the subject", and described a problem that existed in the company whereby the "users who shouted loudest" decided the development priorities and schedule. He believed the method served to create a more professional aura for the IS department—a statement to the effect that "we've got standards for our work, just like other departments". This could then be used to safeguard against being forced to meet unreasonable deadlines.

One of the banks studied was using the Information Engineering method for the early phases of development. The IS manager stated that it had been the case that the IS department were typically consulted in the last stage of the decision cycle when it came to business planning and strategy formulation. He believed the focus of the IS department was too often just reactive to problem situations, whereas there was a need to be more proactive in identifying business opportunities and creating a "business case" to justify and support systems development. Thus, he wanted the IS department to be involved at a much earlier stage in the decision cycle, and by promoting the phases and techniques of Information Engineering which addressed the area of business strategy planning, he was able to promote the IS department role to an earlier one in the planning and strategy formulation process. He was very satisfied with the contribution of Information Engineering, suggesting that almost all of the major development projects recently undertaken in the bank had been underpinned by a business case derived from the application of Information Engineering.

The IS manager in this bank also identified another role that methods can play, namely, that of *confidence factor*. He explained it as follows: management often know intuitively what the business problems and opportunities are, but a proposal to spend a vast sum of money on systems development needs as much justification as possible. Thus, the systematic approach to building a business case, which the Information Engineering method provided, served to provide management with more confidence that the decision was justifiable. That is to say, there was safety and comfort in following the detailed prescriptions of the method in that management could not later vociferously complain about the process followed.

The IS manager in the food processing company identified another similar role that a method can play, namely that of *audit trail*. By documenting all steps of the development process and the rationale behind development decisions, some protection was afforded, since "a decision that's right now, might not be right in the future". This role is closely related to the 'comfort factor.' He described the situation as one whereby management wanted to be provided with systems planning reports; "they will never be read, but they want to have them for safety".

The role of method of legitimising the development process was also evident during our research. The IS manager in one software house described it as "the tail wagging the dog" and suggested it was a phenomenon in their client companies. However, in this software house, the mere fact of having a documented method was acknowledged as useful, and very important for marketing as it could be used to impress clients, and to convince them that there was "quality in the development process". Also, in a food processing company, a major goal within the IS department was to achieve ISO certification, and the method was seen as a way of "organising and focusing minds on ISO".

In one government department, the project leader also expressed a view which supported the notion of a method legitimising the development process, in suggesting that if they wanted to reject a proposal from a sub-contractor, the fact that the sub-contractor was not using SSADM could be a convenient excuse, even if perhaps not the real reason.

Another role that methods can play which was identified during our research was that of power base for the method champions. Given the decentralisation of development into user departments, IS developers have lost some of their traditional power base due to the information knowledge that was in the past associated with systems development. In one food processing company, a project manager was very proud that he was closely identified with the formalisation of the development process. He suggested that there had been "fads of documentation in the past", but now the quest for ISO accreditation was underway, and he was "leading it". Certainly, this interviewee was very positive about the benefits of a method. However, it was a means of raising his profile within the company.

While the rational roles justify the use of formalised methods, the political roles serve to influence the method-in-action in a myriad of ways. For example, in one software house, when development was being done for a government agency client, the official policy would mandate that the SSADM method be used. However, even in this scenario, developers would develop as they saw fit, but later retrofit the documentation to make it appear as if the SSADM method had been followed. Likewise, these developers were sufficiently proficient in Information Engineering to accomplish the same affect if necessary.

5.7   CHAPTER SUMMARY

This chapter has identified a number of factors that support the use of formalised methods, and also a number of pressures for increased formalism in the development process. These factors are quite compelling, but were countered by a set of factors which militate against the use of formalised methods, and a set of pressures for alternative more rapid approaches to ISD. The arguments in favour of the use of methods represent a set of rational roles that methods can overtly play, and there has been considerable support for these factors in the ISD literature, and they are also supported by our own empirical research into ISD. However, we also identified a set of political roles that methods may play. These are more covert and have not been identified in the ISD literature in the past. There was considerable evidence for these covert political factors in our research. It is important for practitioners and researchers to recognise that the assumed role of methods is not as straightforward as it might appear. Reflecting on the various issues discussed in this chapter can contribute to the process of devising the method-in-action.

5.8   DISCUSSION QUESTIONS

1.   Can you think of any other arguments in favour of ISD methods in addition to the ones presented here? Can you think of any other arguments against?
2.   Given the many disadvantages associated with the use of ISD methods, do these outweigh the advantages?
3.   Are the political roles played by methods more significant than the rational intellectual roles? Considering yourself as a practitioner, can you think of any additional political roles?
4.   Do you think the use of formalised ISD methods in practice is on the increase? Should it be?
5.   The quotes from the literature presented in this chapter suggest that academic researchers have a low opinion of ISD practice. Is this justifiable? What do you think is the ISD practitioners' opinion of academic researchers? Think of some suitable quotes!

The Development Context

6.1 INTRODUCTION

The development context is the foundation of information systems development. The importance of awareness and a detailed understanding of the context is emphasised as a vital part of our framework. Some basic aspects of the context and also the relationship between context, technology, culture and change are discussed in this chapter. Also, various ISD change strategies are identified, including proactive versus reactive, problem-solving versus innovation, incremental versus radical, long-term versus short-term, high risk versus low risk (see Fig. 6.1).

6.2 THE DEVELOPMENT CONTEXT

All information systems are situated in a context and developed within a context. Information systems are created, designed and produced for a specific situation or at least a specific type of situation. The context is therefore everything when it comes to information systems—and thus inherently complex. Technology, functionality, usefulness, efficiency, and ease of use are all characteristics of an information system that basically must be evaluated in relation to a specific context. In most cases, the context is some kind of organisation or company. But today we have to be aware of the fact that information systems development also takes place in more

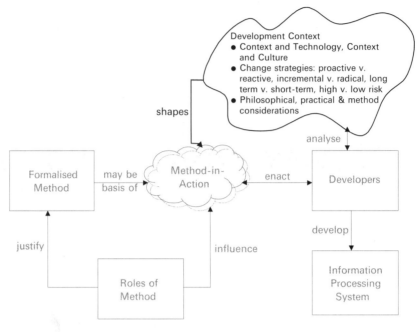

Fig. 6.1   The Development Context

loosely organised contexts. It might be a virtual organisation, or a cluster of organisations, or some informal collaboration between different types of organisations, such as businesses working together with non-profit organisations and government departments.

We define the context as both the place where the information system will be implemented and the environment within which the development process will take place. We are not making any distinction between the context where the development process is conducted and where the outcome will be implemented. The outcome of the development process is a unique system, encompassing not only computers and other technical equipment and software, but also organisational changes such as new work procedures and personnel roles. Yet, even when an information system includes commercial off-the-shelf (COTS) software, the activities of information systems development are performed to determine the system/software requirements and to adapt the product to fit the particular circumstances.

The context, being the destination of the developed system, has several connotations. Firstly, the context is typically perceived as the 'problem situation', i.e. a situation that is problematic and requires change. However, at the same time, the context also affords new business opportunities. These opportunities are present, but perhaps not always visible. A developer has the responsibility to transform the present context, with the help of an information system, into a new and more desirable context. Information system development is all about that kind of transformation.

The context plays an important role in the framework presented in this book. A context, in this framework, is always a unique situation. A context never appears twice. A development project is never dealing twice with the same context or the same system. This means that the context influences all the other parts of the framework. It is the precondition that cannot be chosen. All other parts of the framework can be exchanged or substituted but that is not true for the context. Within a development project it is possible to choose a method, to choose a developer, but it is not possible to choose another context. In this sense the context is the *a priori* background or foundation for the whole development process and for the involved people and technology.

6.3   AWARENESS OF DEVELOPMENT CONTEXT

Within the field of ISD there has not always been an awareness of the importance of the development context. In the early days, and maybe still prevalent in some quarters, was the notion that development of a system should be guided by the principle of the context-free system and the context-free development process. A context-free system was thought of as a system that would perform uniformly in all contexts. Over time that idea has been fundamentally challenged, to the extent that the opposite view has become prominent, namely that of the fully context-dependent system. Viewed from this perspective, it is not possible to simply transform a system from one context to another.

The notion of a context-free development process has also been challenged. This in turn has led to a diversity of development methods. Currently, we can identify highly formalised methods which have been created with a particular type of context in mind—highly structured and formalised contexts such as a manufacturing process industry, for example. It is also possible to identify development methods for highly flexible and dynamic contexts, such as virtual teams or customer-sensitive businesses. The idea that the context heavily influences both what kind of system is needed and what kind of development process is needed has been illustrated repeatedly in the ISD literature.

The history of ISD also shows that what is considered to be context-dependent or not has changed over time. In the early days all systems were developed as highly context-dependent. New systems were developed as in-house specific systems with special attention paid to the requirements of the context at hand. This development was usually done by developers internal to the organisation who had specific knowledge of the everyday routines of the organisation. Over time this situation changed and the use of external consultants from outside the organisation became commonplace. Of course, the reason for using in-house competence or external consultants has changed over time, usually in relation to how technology has evolved.

These factors were also borne out in our empirical research into this topic. In one survey, we found that the use of formalised ISD methods was significantly higher in larger organisations (more than 1000 employees), and in larger IS departments (more than 20 personnel). This is in keeping with the project management role that methods play (as discussed in Chapter 5), and would suggest that they facilitate intercommunication among developers and help control long projects. This survey also indicated that method usage was very significantly associated with both high levels of in-house development and low levels of customisation of packages and development outsourced. Additionally, the survey revealed that methods were significantly more likely to be used when more than five developers were involved on the project, and when the project duration was greater than 9 months.

Our survey findings were confirmed in subsequent interviews. For example, one pharmaceutical company who were not very formalised in their development approach had the smallest IS department (six personnel) and were doing the least amount of in-house development (20 per cent) with quite a short project duration (3 months) and about two developers working on a typical project. On the other hand, the organisations with the most formalised approaches, the banks, software houses, and government departments, all tended to have larger development teams and to have longer project duration. In contrast, the project leader in a public utility company suggested that project duration of 2 to 10 days was very common. He had used a formalised method in a company in which he had worked previously, but acknowledged that projects had been of longer duration and the environment more formal.

These studies show that development is to a large extent influenced by the context in which it takes place. There are a lot of factors that have to be taken into account in the planning of the development process. An awareness of these factors must be in place to inform the choice of approach and method.

6.3.1   Context and Technology

One of the most crucial questions that needs to be considered in all contexts is the relationship between changes in context and changes in technology. Today, almost every organisation is challenged to some extent by new technology. New technological advancements make it possible to perform organisational tasks in a different way. At the same time, the internal competence changes within organisations, new ways of doing things are developed, new products are invented, new ways of utilising existing skills, materials, and services evolve.

Given the ever-changing technology and context, the question as to which should be the motivation for change is a very complex one, and one which does not get easier over time. Different organisations choose different strategies. Some decide to use the latest technological advances as the primary motivation for change. These organisations are always looking for new technology that might change the way they do their 'business'. The guiding principle seems to be that whenever a new technology appears it is important to be among the first to take advantage of it. This forces the organisation to change to accommodate the new technology. Other organisations view their internal way of doing things as the core. This means that development is thought of as based on internal competence and procedures. Technology is seen as a tool that should be adapted or shaped in accordance with that competence and procedures.

Two examples which illustrate these different strategies are Amazon and FedEx. In the Amazon case, technology was the primary organisational motivator. Company founder Jeff Bezos defied the conventional wisdom which suggests that one should begin with a business case and then investigate how technology could best support that business case. Rather, he perceived the Internet and Web as technologies with enormous potential to revolutionise business. Given this technology-afforded potential, his quest became that of selecting the type of business that could best leverage this technology. He concluded that the book retail market was the best bet. The Amazon model represents a paradigm shift from the general book retailing model which requires distributors and fixed premises—bricks and mortar—to sell books. The rest is, as they say, history. Amazon became the defining example of exploitation of the new technology, to the extent that it was seen as the 'killer application' for the Internet era. That is, just as the electronic spreadsheet was the killer application which motivated huge numbers of people to buy personal computers in the 1980s, thousands of people have purchased Internet connections principally because they wanted to access Amazon in the late 1990s.

An example of a company that have taken the existing context as primary and have used technology to refine the organisation is FedEx. This is a company whose core competence is that of a postal service. FedEx is the defining example of a company who have been able to adapt new technology to their core competence, and in doing so, making it more efficient and service-oriented. The basic procedures, however, are still the same, i.e. handling and shipping of letters and packages.

Depending on how the relationship between technology and context is understood, different strategies for development can be adopted. Thus, it is important for an organisation to reflect upon that relationship and to develop an intentional strategy upon which information systems development can be based.

6.3.2   Context and Culture

Within every organisation there is a culture. This culture is something developed over time and is a collection of experiences expressed in a set of beliefs and values. Over time these beliefs and values will be 'inscribed' in the procedures and processes used within the organisation—a culture is then in place.

Sometimes a culture is something explicitly espoused, and sometimes it is there but not easily visible. A culture will influence what is and what is not possible to do within a specific context. Traditional norms and values will make certain approaches to change more or less feasible or appropriate. In some cultures there is a strong emphasis on administration and bureaucracy. In others, there is a tradition of flexibility and individual freedom. Some cultures are a result of pre-defined conditions and it is not possible to change them—the requirement to comply with legal constraints, for example. Others are based on unique local requirements—security issues where the well-being of humans is at stake, for example.

Organisational cultures have a strong influence on how information systems development can be approached. To understand the context as a culture, and to understand what kind of development approaches may be appropriate or not within a context is in many cases a precondition for being successful.

6.4   STRATEGIES FOR CHANGE

Within every context there is a tradition and culture of how to approach change, and there are diverse strategies by which information systems may be employed to achieve change. These different strategies for change are not easily defined and are, of course, in reality always blended. In this section, we will briefly discuss some of the more common approaches to change, expressed here as dichotomous strategies that operate in tension to each other.

6.4.1   Proactive versus Reactive

One of the most visible tensions is that between a proactive and a reactive strategy. A proactive development process is one that is not initiated in reaction to a problem in the existing situation. Rather, an opportunity might present itself that can be exploited by means of a new information system. In ISD, the far more common case is a reactive strategy, that is, development is initiated to address some problem in the existing situation. A proactive strategy is a way to get ahead, to change a context before problems arise and before change is just a way to take care of immediate problems. It is thus a way to move in an intentional direction. In contrast, the reactive approach is one where change is triggered by events elsewhere. It is when the environment or the preconditions for the context have changed in ways that makes a certain action necessary. To be reactive means that the choice of action is not present, and it is to move in a direction decided by someone else.

In our empirical research, in one of the banks, the IS manager elaborated on

existing. Therefore, there is no single correct or true answer to the question 'What systems should we develop?' The answer to this question cannot be found merely by studying the context. There are methods that stress the analysis of the context to such an extent that it seems they presuppose that the answer may be found through careful analysis. A good example of this type of philosophy can be gleaned from the Structured Approach (discussed in Chapter 3), where two of its leading advocates, McMenamin & Palmer, boldly contend that "the specification should contain all the true requirements and nothing but the true requirements" McMenamin & Palmer, 1984, p. 77).

Careful analysis is always valuable and is of great help in the development process but it is not enough. From a philosophical standpoint, the system that is developed is always a result of someone's imagination and judgement. Based on this, the issue of knowing how to study the context and to what extent is always a result of judgement based on specific aspects of the context. It can only be answered in relation to why the knowledge is needed.

6.5.2   Practical Considerations

Apart from the philosophical consideration, there is also a practical issue. To study a context in detail, to find out how everything works, how and why people behave in the way they do, how and why processes and structures look the way they do, can be an eternal endeavour. There is no end to the amount of information and knowledge that can be created from careful analysis of a context, so much so that the phrase 'paralysis by analysis' has been coined to describe this phenomenon. This means that for very practical purposes it is extremely important to know what to study and why.

If inquiries are to be practical, they have to be guided by judgement and intention. Thus, the study of the context has to be guided by a purpose and also by an idea of what the intention behind a new information system might be. As a consequence, some initial idea of the outcome has to be in place when the analysis starts. In interviews with project leaders they answered the question as to when the first idea emerges:

> *Actually the first time you meet the problem or the persons involved*

> *I think it is done very early, too early, before the analysis begins you think about how to solve it, unfortunately.*

It seems as if they viewed this as a problem. When asked why they saw it as a problem, they answered that it was the opposite of what the methods told them to do. One project manager replied:

> *You are supposed to begin the analysis of the company without any preconceived ideas, but that is never the case.*

Another one commented:

> *According to methods you are supposed to analyse reality first and based on that draw your conclusions, I think it seldom works like that, because you know in advance what you want.*

The way they describe the process does suggest that they are capable of making intentional choices on what to analyse and how detailed the analysis has to be, since they have an initial first idea that guides their judgement. If this were not the case, a context analysis would take forever since there would be no condition that would inform the developer to decide when sufficient analysis has taken place. What constitutes sufficient knowledge about the context is therefore always dependent on the intended system and the strategies chosen for the development process.

6.5.3 Method Considerations

A context is unique. How to study a context in a methodical way is therefore also uniquely related to the context at hand. It is possible to use the same method to study different contexts, but it cannot be done without some kind of customising or tailoring of the method, that is a method-in-action must be configured based on the requirements of the context (see Chapter 9).

If the context in question is an organisation with a lot of complex social relationships—a service-oriented organisation such as an insurance company, for instance—the method adopted must reflect that specific situation. An insurance company, as a context, is very different from a manufacturing process industry such as a paper mill. Both are examples of organisations of high complexity, but of a very different nature. Social complexity is not the same thing as technical complexity. The difference between these two contexts have implications for the ISD methods used.

Complexity is only one aspect that might vary between contexts. There are other aspects, such as how fast they change over time, how much they rely on technology, how knowledge within the field develops, etc. In all these cases the developer has to make a judgement as to how the characteristics of the context should influence the approach and method chosen.

6.6 CHAPTER SUMMARY

In this chapter we have discussed the importance of the context element in the overall framework of information systems development. Every context is unique. And unlike the other parts of the framework, there is no degree of freedom when it comes to the context. This means that the context will influence all other decision made in relation to a development process. We mentioned that this is the case with the choice of method, but it is also the case with the developer.

Every context demands some kind of specific knowledge and skill. A developer usually develops his or her skill in relation to a certain domain of practice. Developers become over time knowledgeable with a special expertise in, for instance, banking, manufacturing, government agencies, or maybe even more specific domains, such as, accounting or booking systems.

In relation to the framework, the context is the foundation. An awareness of the role and importance of the context is crucial to all kinds of ISD. Developers need to develop knowledge on how to understand, approach and deal with contexts. They also need to know how to recognise characteristics in different contexts that are of special importance for the development process. We move a discussion of the developer component next.

6.7   DISCUSSION QUESTIONS

1.   ISD always takes place within a context. Are there situations where context awareness might actually be more of a hindrance than a help?
2.   How does the relationship between new technology and the development context create concerns for the developer? And how can that be handled?
3.   There are many strategies for change. Can you come up with any other strategies besides the ones mentioned in the book?
4.   To what extent is the developer responsible for having an adequate understanding of the context? And what are the basic strategies for creating such an understanding?
5.   In the chapter the uniqueness of the context is stated as fundamental to ISD. What consequences does this have on the competence and skills required in a developer? How can this be addressed in the education of developers?

7

Developers

7.1   INTRODUCTION

This chapter considers the role of the actual developers in IS development. In our framework, developers are accorded a central role, as it is an inescapable fact that it is people not methods who develop systems, and that methods are at best an organising mechanism that should support developers. Thus, the importance in the development process of developer-embodied factors is explicitly acknowledged. These are leveraged by the developer during development and, as the framework in Fig. 7.1 illustrates, are drawn upon by the developer to analyse the development context, uniquely enact the method-in-action, and develop the actual information processing system. A number of specific developer-related factors have been identified, based on both previous ISD research, and also our own empirical research into the topic. These include capabilities of individual developers, actual method use by developers, developer as designer, knowledge of the application domain, developer commitment and motivation, and developer autonomy. Each of these is discussed in more detail in this chapter.

7.2   THE IMPORTANCE OF THE INDIVIDUAL DEVELOPER

IS development has long been problematic, and since the software crisis term was first coined in 1968, there has been a belief that the solution might lie in more engineering like approaches to ISD. This has led to the creation and promulgation of various

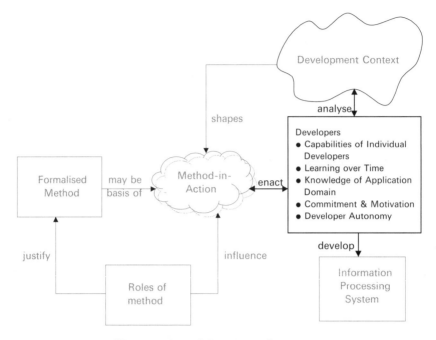

Fig. 7.1 The IS Developer Component

idealised ISD methods that attempt to capture an engineering-like approach (see Chapters 3 and 4). The spirit of this profound belief in method is well captured by Colter (1982) who praised the contribution of ISD methods for moving the field "from the old artsy processes," while lamenting the fact that "much is still left to the abilities of the designer". Thus, formalised methods seek to eliminate any reliance on individual developer ability. For example, one of the explicit goals of the Jackson Systems Development (JSD) method was to eliminate personal creativity from the development process. Indeed, one of the stated benefits of the method was that it reduced reliance on developer inspiration and creativity, and could and should be applied in the same way by all developers in all situations (King & Pardoe, 1985). In a similar fashion, more recently, the CMM approach seeks to avoid the necessity for relying on individual heroics as a means of achieving successful IS development (cf. Bach, 1994; Paulk *et al.*, 1993).

However, the importance of individual developer ability has long been acknowledged in ISD research. Boehm (1981) reported that people factors have more than six times greater effect on development productivity than the use of any software tools. Brooks (1987) held a similar position, and recommended that processes be put in place to nourish creative people. He argued that few fields have such a large gap between best current practice and average practice. In support of this conclusion,

Glass (1991) reported differences of up to 30 to 1 between developers. That is, some developers were 30 times more productive than others.

Furthermore, Brooks (1987) suggested that systems development is a creative process and that a method cannot "inspire the drudge". The ingenuity and ability of the developer cannot be compounded into any ISD method. Rather, it is more likely the case that strict adherence to a method may actually preclude innovation.

Our empirical research into ISD has also confirmed the importance of individual developer ability. It was evident in all the organisations studied that the different skills and aptitudes of individual developers were very relevant when allocating development responsibility. The typical policy was to recruit and develop product specialists who would take ownership and assume responsibility for these specialist areas.

7.3   DEVELOPER AS DESIGNER

The development of an information system is a design task, meaning that it is basically a creative and compositional process. The skills needed and the abilities drawn upon are many and varied. In our empirical studies and especially in interviews with system developers and project managers we have found certain aspects of the design ability to be at the core. It is possible to summarise these abilities as a kind of intelligence characterised by being compositional and intentional. Even though these aspects are readily apparent in empirical research, they are seldom discussed in the literature on ISD methods. It seems as if the ability of the individual developer is not traditionally viewed as important enough.

In our research, it became apparent that developers have an understanding of what is expected from them with regard to abilities and skills. We will briefly discuss some of these abilities. The primary purpose is to illustrate the complexity of skills that developers are challenged with. Another purpose is to make clear some of the aspects of information systems development not usually dealt with in a methodical way. Methods focus on creating a framework for the process, and on specifying procedures, techniques, and tools. There is not the same attention given to the developer who is the one charged with making it all happen.

It is frequently assumed that the developer has to be rational. Even though this seems an intuitive expression, it is not commonly defined in a way that reveals what kind of ability this actually entails. Sometimes, to be rational refers to doing the right thing in an efficient and logical way. This is how being rational is often described in formalised methods. When it comes to practitioners, the basic understanding of rationality is another matter. To them it refers to the notion that an act or decision has to be possible to understand. When we understand the rationale behind an action, we can label that action as rational. To be rational in design is not so much about being efficient, as it is about communication. One of the very crucial abilities for a developer is to be able to communicate with clients and users. In our research this was mentioned as probably the most important ability of all. The developer has to act and express himself in a rational way to be understood. The development process is to a large extent about communication. A 'rational' developer is one that acts in a way that clients and users understand.

Another aspect of communication within a project is the large disparity in knowledge about technology and context among clients, users and developers. The pedagogical skills needed by developers are therefore both real and vital.

In our studies we have also found that developers, in reflecting on their abilities, consider both creative and analytic skills as fundamental. It is not unusual to frame these two types of skills as contradictory. In our everyday experience we usually characterise people as either creative or analytical. System developers seem to perceive both skills as needed simultaneously. They are referred to as necessary throughout the whole process, at all times.

One of the most vital, and at the same time most elusive, abilities is that of compositional skill. This is the skill to come up with a new system and to imagine how this system and the existing context can be composed into a whole system. The compositional skill is needed even in the case where the system comprises packaged software. According to experienced developers this ability to imagine and compose the final total system is a result of creative and analytical thinking. In the first phases of an information systems development project, the new system only exists as an imaginary abstract concept. To be a good developer means to be able to create an image of something not yet existing, in a way that makes it both 'visible' and understandable to non-technologically skilled people.

A new system, in a complex context, is extremely difficult to imagine, taking into consideration all its implications and consequences. This leads to the conclusion that imagination, in relation to the ability to be systemic, is necessary when dealing with complex compositions of social and technical systems.

Finally, all the difficult challenges that face a developer are never to be solved by straightforward technical solutions. There is no way to measure if a system is the 'correct' or 'true' solution for a specific context. There is no correct way to imagine, visualise, communicate, create, analyse, or compose a new system. The developer's final skill is judgement. The ability to exercise good judgement is at the very core of all design processes. Judgement is usually not something accorded high prominence in methods. The reverse is usually the case in fact. That is, when something cannot be handled in a methodical manner, it is often omitted from the prescriptive method. To do justice to the complexity of information systems development and the role of the developer, concepts like the ones discussed above should be addressed in an intentional and serious way. Maybe the most important influence on the development process could be achieved by focusing on such elusive but vital aspects. It is obvious though, that to practising developers, these aspects of the development process and their own role are very real.

7.4   DEVELOPER AND METHOD USE

Use Formalised methods do not allow for the learning and experience that developers gain over time. Each systems development project is generally undertaken as if it was unique. Yet, in a comparative study of successful and unsuccessful systems analysts, Vitalari & Dickson (1983) emphasised the importance of learning over time. They concluded that developers acquired a "repertoire of strategies" to apply in different system development situations. This is in accord with Davis & Olson (1985) who suggested that developers gain more domain knowledge over time and that this is a vital factor in successful system development. To view system development as an orderly progression from requirements analysis to a solution designed purely around those requirements is to miss the critical synergy between developer and user. Both the developer and user learn through a dialectic approach, in that by hearing about potential capabilities of the system, users envisage new features. Vitalari & Dickson (1983) also argued that successful designers learn a great deal through trial and error. Therefore, an idealised approach to system development as portrayed in a formalised method may be seriously flawed since it omits the fact that failure is essential to human learning. In calling for a paradigm change in how ISD is conceptualised, Floyd (1987) criticised product-oriented methods as static rule-systems operating in a stereotyped, standardised manner. She called for a process-oriented perspective with a central role for the learning process, where methods:

> appear as second-order learning processes, based on an ever-growing class of individual past learning processes in actual projects, using guidelines offered by method authors and tailored to the situation in hand, and preparing us for future learning processes in developing software.

Certainly, the manner in which individual developers built up their knowledge over time was a recurring theme in our empirical research. In one software house, the IS manager put it as follows:

> a couple of our payroll guys know the whole system, even though it's as big as Encyclopaedia Britannica

Two interesting related issues which arise in the ISD literature in relation to method usage are the following: Firstly, whether the low level of method use (which has been widely reported) is primarily due to ignorance on the part of developers, as has been suggested. Secondly, there are differing views as to whether experienced developers are more or less likely to use methods. For example, some researchers (e.g. Leonard-Barton, 1987) suggested that experienced developers were more likely to use methods, the argument being that they realise the benefits of using methods. However, other researchers have reported less use of methods among experienced developers (e.g. Kozar, 1989; Lee & Kim, 1992). We investigated these issues in our empirical research.

7.4.1   Developer Awareness of Methods

The evidence from our research suggests that ignorance is not an explanatory factor for low levels of usage of formalised ISD methods in practice. Several of the organisations studied had purchased and evaluated various commercial formalised methods, and received the requisite training. This would suggest that any decision not to use these methods was based on a position of knowledge rather than ignorance. Indeed, one organisation explained their rejection of a particular formalised method as being due to the fact that it was "incredibly cumbersome" and not at all suited to the needs of their environment.

7.4.2   Developer Experience and Method Usage

There are conflicting views as to whether development experience is positively correlated with method usage or not. The argument in favour of positive correlation suggests that experienced developers will realise the benefits that a method provides and will use it. The argument against suggests that experienced developers will find a method constraining and are more likely to step outside it, whereas novice or inexperienced developers will use a method due to the complexity of ISD. This latter argument received some support in our empirical research. For example, one IS manager expressed the view that "experienced developers find a method a bit of a hindrance," while another stated that "experienced developers could be completely fettered by methods." One project leader summarised both views by stating that "the younger want something to lean against, while the older and more experienced don't have the same need".

It was suggested that new developers are now quite amenable to following formalised methods as they may have been exposed to them as part of their education, in contrast to developers in the past, many of whom typically acquired their development skills through practice, without any formal training.

From this evidence, one might conclude that method usage is negatively correlated with developer experience. However, methods were being used by experienced developers in the organisations we studied. Developers did sometimes depart from the method, but in a conscious and deliberate fashion. One IS manager suggested that experienced developers do not object to method guidelines that make sense. This

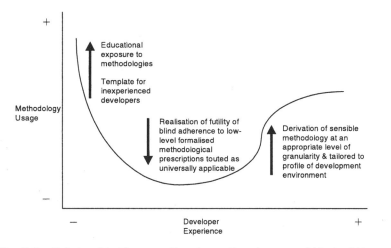

Fig. 7.2   Relationship Between Developer Experience and Method Usage

theme was echoed in several organisations. A project manager in charge of implementation of a formalised method stated that he did not consider there to be resistance from experienced developers to the method; rather, he described it as a "challenge" from developers, who initially questioned the proposed method, but, once persuaded of the benefits of the method, were happy to accept it.

A common scenario was reported in a government department, where the IS manager suggested that inexperienced developers would follow a method because of uncertainty or lack of confidence. However, once they gained some experience, they tended to take more chances and follow an informal development approach. However, they eventually came to realise the negative implications of not following certain aspects of the method, and came around to increased method usage.

Thus, a U-shaped curve seems to capture the relationship between developer experience and method usage, as depicted in Fig. 7.2. However, the interview evidence would suggest some mediating factors or pressures. Firstly, educational exposure to methods might predispose inexperienced developers more towards a formalised approach. Also, inexperienced developers could find that a method provides a useful template for the development process. Subsequently, the realisation of the futility of blind and slavish adherence to low-level standards, prescribed as universally applicable, could cause developers to make less use of methods. Thus, method use would appear to go down over time as developers gain more experience, thus perhaps explaining some of the findings of negative correlation of developer experience and method use. Eventually, the derivation of a tailored method-in-action which provides sensible standards and guidelines at the appropriate level of granularity could predispose experienced developers towards increased method usage.

7.5   KNOWLEDGE OF APPLICATION DOMAIN

In a similar fashion, formalised methods do not allow for the knowledge of the application domain that developers bring to the ISD equation. This philosophy is certainly not in accord with the widely held view that developer knowledge of the application domain is one of the most important factors in ensuring successful system development.

In our empirical research into this topic, one of the banks we studied had experienced a high turnover of staff, which is not that unusual in the IT industry, but was unusual for this bank. They had lost five developers in the previous year, but believed this was a one-time occurrence. The developers who left had been recruited directly as university graduates. However, the staff structures in the IS department mirrored those of the rest of the bank, and some of these graduates were not willing to wait for career advancement which could take several years. The bank had decided to revert to their previous policy of recruiting employees from the bank branches based on their performance on IT aptitude tests. This had the two-fold advantage of recruiting both those who were apparently satisfied with the existing staff structures, and who also already had experience of the banking business domain. This knowledge was seen as critical and these recruits were then trained in the technical areas of IS development.

We also investigated the issue of technical expertise versus application domain expertise. In the organisations studied, most interviewees felt that both were vital—"the ideal developer has both" according to the IS manager in one software house. Interestingly, IS managers tended to rate knowledge of the business domain higher, whereas the more hands-on developers tended to rate technical expertise higher. However, the issue was put in perspective by the IS managers in two of the organisations: In a pharmaceutical company, the IS manager felt that technical expertise was becoming less important due to technological advances which were making the technology more transparent. Likewise in one of the banks, it was felt that a particular *threshold* level of technical expertise was required, and once this was achieved, business domain knowledge became increasingly important. This notion of a threshold level of technical expertise received support from interviewees in the other organisations also.

7.6   DEVELOPER COMMITMENT AND MOTIVATION

Developer commitment and motivation has not featured prominently in ISD research in the past. However, it is obviously related to the developer ability factor mentioned above. In our empirical research, this factor has loomed large, with the importance of developer commitment and motivation being emphasised in all the organisations studied. Interviewees repeatedly expressed the view that development was not a nine-to-five job, and that work in the evening and at weekends was inevitable.

Commitment and motivation were viewed as far more important than actual technical expertise.

In all but two of the organisations studied, there was very low turnover of IT staff, much lower than one would expect in the IT sector generally. In one food processing company, several developers were commuting exceptionally long distances to work. However, the IS manager stressed the motivational aspects of working on exciting new development projects using the latest technologies. This issue was stressed in several other organisations also. For example, the IS manager in one software house felt that assigning responsibility and giving people ownership of systems was a good motivator also. Additionally, in one of the banks, the opportunity to work more closely with top management was identified as a significant motivation. In one government department, it transpired that IS experience was seen as "good on the CV", and thus, a posting to the IS department was enthusiastically sought and ensured motivation among those who worked there.

Another related factor which emerged in our research as being relevant was that of *trust* in individual developers. This manifested itself internally in organisations where, given the intimate knowledge of developer aptitudes, it was often the case that trusted developers were assigned responsibility for particular critical development tasks and projects. However, trust was a factor in external relationships also, with some organisations allocating vital development roles to external specialists whose contribution was an essential component of development in these organisations.

7.7 DEVELOPER AUTONOMY

In the early days of computing, developers were typically scientists who were developing programs for themselves. In such an environment, these developers operated in an environment of "responsible autonomy," to use Friedman's (1989) term. In the interim, there have been efforts to impose more control on developers. However, an interesting finding emerged from a study by DeMarco & Lister (1989) which showed that even in organisations where methods were supposedly rigidly enforced, there was very poor convergence on design style among different developers. This reinforces the point that development methods cannot be inflicted on developers.

In our empirical research, we also found quite a lot of evidence of "responsible autonomy" on the part of developers. In one public utility company, a project leader indicated that project management roles were fluid, in that regardless of actual title, different individuals assumed project management roles depending on the area. Also, he stated that hierarchies had blurred in the IS department to the extent that an informal environment prevailed whereby developers, regardless of position or title, had quite a degree of autonomy in relation to recommending changes in development practices. A developer in one of the government departments stated that even though the SSADM method (see Chapter 3 above) was recommended within the organisation, developers had absolute discretion in relation to the development process. However, he acknowledged that this led to certain problems in development, as some tasks might not be completed—documentation, for example. Thus, the issue of trust in individual developers, mentioned above, is quite an important factor.

7.8   CRITICAL ROLE OF DEVELOPER

Based on the above discussion of developer factors, we can conclude that even though developers are seldom accorded adequate recognition in formalised methods, they do have a critical role in the development process, but it is also obvious that developer abilities cannot be formally prescribed in the form of methods.

One major role that the developer plays is a consequence of the limitations of formalised methods. Formalised methods have to be carefully evoked to become methods-in-action. This has to be done with regard to the unique aspects of the development context. But this has another consequence. It means that it is not possible to act in the same way twice. There are never two identical projects. A developer cannot use experience as a source for action; experience can only inform and prepare for action.

The role of the developer is therefore not to have ready-made solutions or judgements. Everything has to be done in the particular situation. A really good developer, open to the complexity and uniqueness of the specific situation, must be prepared. To be prepared means to have a sense of the unique, to be able to adapt techniques and methods to the particular needs and demands, to be able to see the specifics of the context, and to make good judgements based on all this.

In his books on the "reflective practitioner," Donald Schön makes a strong case for the skilled practitioner as a person who is prepared to deal with messy real world situations, and not a person with "technical rationality". Technical rationality is the approach to problem solving based on scientific knowledge. Schön argues for the artistry approach which is based on continuous reflection in action. Skilled designers can act based on their judgement skills, and at the same time also prepare for the next situation by having a reflective approach to the situation, their own skills and abilities, needs and demands, etc.

With regard to the complexity of skills involved and the changing preconditions for development, artistry is involved in information systems development. But it is artistry that has to be based on a solid foundation of knowledge about technology and social issues. The abilities needed are constantly changing and a developer will never be fully competent. One of the best investments in the process of information systems development is that of focusing on the developers and their continuous competence improvement. All our studies show that there are radical differences in outcomes among developers. We are also convinced that these differences cannot be eliminated simply by applying methods. When it comes to method-in-action, the developer has the leading role. The developer breathes life into methods and techniques and it is their abilities and skills that make the important difference in the final outcome.

7.9   CHAPTER SUMMARY

This chapter considered the importance of developers and developer-embodied factors in IS development. Among the factors discussed were the capabilities of individual developers, as these are by far the most significant factor in successful ISD, notwithstanding the fact that many formalised methods strive to eliminate any reliance on developer ability.

The chapter also examined the importance of developer learning over time, including the fact that lessons learned from ISD failure may be extremely useful in the learning process. The issue of whether the low level of usage of ISD methods, reported in many studies, might be due to ignorance on the part of developers was also considered, and the conclusion based on our research was that this was not actually the case; rather developers were tailoring methods, or pragmatically omitting steps on the basis of what might work best given the contingencies of the development context. The apparent paradox as to whether developer experience is positively or negatively correlated with method usage was also considered. In this case, the evidence suggests that novice developers are likely to follow a method, and that very experienced developers are also likely to follow a method. However, the method is very different in each case. The novice developers are likely to enact a method-in-action which is quite similar to an actual formalised method, whereas experienced developers will enact a method-in-action which is better suited to their skills and ability, the actual needs of the development context, and the system under development.

Another developer factor considered in this chapter was knowledge of the application business domain, a factor not explicitly acknowledged in formalised methods. The organisations studied tended to view business knowledge of the application domain as more important than any technical expertise, and viewed the latter as something in which a particular threshold level could be achieved quite readily with training, whereas business expertise in the application domain was something which took far longer to acquire.

Developer commitment and motivation is another factor that is quite under-researched in the ISD literature. However, these were found to be very important in the organisations studied. It was generally felt that commitment and motivation arose from a number of sources. For example, the experience of working on projects with new technology was cited as a significant motivator, as was the opportunity to work more closely with top management. Another factor that emerged as being relevant was that of trust in individual developers. This manifested itself internally in organisations where, given the intimate knowledge of developer aptitudes, it was often the case that trusted developers were assigned responsibility for particular critical development tasks and projects. However, trust was a factor in external relationships also, with some organisations allocating vital development roles to external specialists whose contribution was an essential component of development in these organisations.

Another developer-related factor considered in this chapter was that of developer autonomy. This was the mode of organising in the early days of computing when the actual developers were scientists developing applications for themselves. Despite efforts over the years to impose stricter control on actual developers, it appears that a large degree of autonomy still prevails in relation to how developers actually go about the development task in practice.

In summary, we believe in the capability of the human developer as an enormous contribution to ISD, a view becoming more widely shared in recent times. However, there have always been those who have resisted attempts to engineer the human out of the ISD equation. An excellent example of an early, albeit cautious, questioning of the role of methods was that of Bubenko (1986 p. 299) who put the case for prominence of softer people issues in the systems development context:

> We should realise that a design will always have an artistic component and that not everything can be 'prescribed' ... the quality of a design is totally dependent on the competence of the designer to the extent that one sometimes wonders about the utility of using a method at all.

The importance of the developer cannot be over-emphasised. Information systems development has as its core the abilities of the people involved especially the developers. The developers use their judgement to bring formalised methods to life by enacting the unique method-in-action for each development context.

7.10   DISCUSSION QUESTIONS

1.   What are the pros and cons of being a developer with deep and specialised knowledge versus having a broader understanding?
2.   What might be good strategies for a developer to adopt in order to maintain autonomy and integrity as a professional?
3.   What is the role of the developer when it comes to the ISD process, and especially the design and planning of that process? And where does this leave the developer in relation to other stakeholders?

4.   To what extent should a developer know specific methods and techniques?
5.   Discuss the role of the developer in relation to the framework presented in the book. What parts and aspects of the framework are or should be the responsibility of the developer?
6.   What are the most important competence and skills in ISD today? What do you think will characterise the information systems developer of the future?

8

Information Processing Systems

8.1   INTRODUCTION

Information systems development is aimed at the design, production and implementation of a system in a context. This chapter focuses on the outcome of this process, namely the resulting information system. The chapter presents a number of ways an information system can be categorised, described and understood. We believe that an awareness of the richness and diversity of systems is important for information systems development. Some of the topics covered here include families of systems, systems and change, and systems-driven development. The relationship between the system and the other parts of the framework are also discussed (see Fig. 8.1).

What constitutes an information system can never be fully defined. The variety and the richness of differences are infinite. Traditionally systems have been categorised by size, or perhaps by computing platform. Historically systems were defined as mainframe systems, mini-computer systems, or micro-computer systems. These distinctions are seldom used today. Another way of describing different kinds of systems is by focusing on who is using the system, such as systems for personal use, for group/team use, organisational use or inter-organisational use. These distinctions are of course relevant, but we do not find them to be sufficient to cater for the complexity of systems development. A more elaborated notion of systems can support the choice of method, determine what kind of competence and skill is necessary, how to deal with the context at hand, etc. The system to be developed, even if it does not exist when the process begins, can have a substantial influence on the development process.

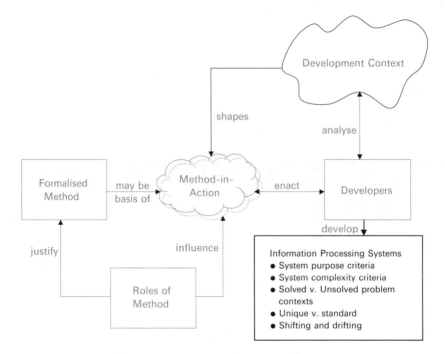

Fig. 8.1   Information Processing Systems

The need for an understanding of systems *per se* is also recognised by practitioners. In one of our studies a project manager stated:

I don't really know myself what signifies good quality in a system ... research can help us a lot here. What is a system really − it is so abstract, you can't really see the result of your work, that is, the system itself, only some kind of reflection.

To reach an understanding of systems requires some kind of language or concepts that make it possible to distinguish types of systems and their characteristics. With such distinctions, choices can be made as to what type of systems to develop, what fits the context at hand, and how to approach the development process.

The chapter begins by discussing different *families of systems*. Even if every system is in some sense unique, there are similarities between systems. Such similarities can be understood as families of systems. Systems are never developed and implemented once and for all. Rather, systems always change. These changes have implications for the development process as well and we will discuss some of these implications. Even if we have chosen to use the notion of families of systems, we have decided not to present these as a list or table. The reason for this is twofold. First, the ongoing technological development itself continuously presents us with new constructions that change the pre-conditions for any kind of comprehensive description. Secondly, we believe that a continuous reflection on types of systems, new categories, and new aspects is at the core of being a professional developer. We hope this chapter can evoke such reflections and lead to a deeper understanding of systems in a long-term perspective. The chapter also discusses external 'forces' that influence the way systems are to be developed and how they behave in the context in which they are deployed, for instance, technology development and external policies. The chapter ends with a discussion of how the information system influences the framework presented in the book and how that affects methods and the use of methods.

8.2   FAMILIES OF SYSTEMS

In everyday life in developed countries today, one encounters all kinds of information systems. Most of us have some kind of contact with a bank, an insurance company, a travel agency, some governmental offices, and many more. All these organisations today use information systems and we are affected by these systems. Either we use some of their systems ourselves through some web interface, or we encounter their systems indirectly by the written information sent to us by regular mail. Today, a lot of people also use the Internet for communication, work or pleasure. All these systems are part of our everyday experience. If we include those systems which are present within workplaces, the number and diversity increases drastically. Most workplaces today are dependent on information systems and some cannot even exist without them. In industry there are a large number of systems that are only visible within the specific organisation, such as systems controlling chemical or production processes, systems for measuring, calculating, evaluating materials, structures, constructions. In these settings, systems are mostly used for handling other systems. Every day, new types of information systems are developed and added to the palette of existing ones.

At the beginning of the development process it is critical to understand the characteristics of the system-to-be in order to know what kind of development process to plan for. With a safety critical system, such as a system governing a nuclear power plant, the development process probably has to be designed to be highly structured and controlled. In this case, a development process which produces a system with unanticipated consequences is not appropriate. On the other hand, if a company is looking for competitive business advantage through a new and radical use of information systems, the process has to be designed to foster creativity and new ways of thinking. Studies have shown significant differences between development processes. Small media and entertainment-oriented development companies have a radically different strategy and organisation in comparison to large engineering companies. So, the purpose of the developed system is an important category.

8.2.1   System Purpose

Even if research has shown that developing different systems requires different approaches, most methods are still promoted as suited to generic or general usage. There are many ways to categorise systems, such as open, closed, adaptive, interactive, natural, living, complex, chaotic systems, etc. Many of these labels are based on a formal or even scientific understanding of the fundamental quality of a system. For most developers the notion of the purpose of the intended system is much more practical and relevant, i.e. what is the core purpose that the developed system has to respond to.

Most people understand the difference between a system developed for the purpose of *entertainment*, such as a computer game, and a system developed for *efficiency*, such as a payroll system. Between these two categories there are major differences in which aspects of the system stand out. In a system for efficiency, key aspects are simplicity in structure, controls for errors, and a simple basic structure, thus making speed a core value. In an entertainment system, the user interface, the experience of playing, built-in surprises and challenges are probably welcome characteristics. But these two purposes are not the only ones possible.

Information technology is frequently used for *control* purposes—systems for control of nuclear power plants, traffic flow, or financial transactions, for example. The possibility of developing information systems that are closely connected in real-time to activities in our real world, and to collect such information, store it, and manipulate it, makes the technology a powerful tool for surveillance in different forms. When these systems can also react to the retrieved information, we get a system with synergistic features. A traffic system that not only keeps track of traffic flow but also re-directs traffic by the use of signals and street signs becomes a part of reality. The system can be in control of reality. The way new information systems are becoming part of our reality in this way increases and fundamentally changes our understanding of information systems. They are no longer only 'tools' that can be used in our organisations when we find them appropriate, they become a real part of the organisation.

One of the most popular ways of using information systems is when they are used to support search, exploration, navigation and orientation in information spaces, such as libraries and database systems. Since information technology has made it possible to store and manage enormous amounts of information, without the under-lying technology it would be impossible to reach and find information needed. Closely related to information-oriented systems are perhaps the largest family of systems—systems for communication. These forms of system are not only important in them-selves, they can also be seen as the glue that brings all other systems together. Systems for communication cover a whole field of systems, from technical systems communicating with other technical systems, to social communication systems. Educational systems are yet another type which possess very different qualities.

Even though we have discussed several different purposes for systems, there are many more. The purpose here is not to present a complete set of categories covering all possible situations. Probably this is not even possible, since technology and development presents us all the time with new systems, for purposes we have not yet even anticipated.

Unfortunately, research into these different kinds of systems has tended to treat them as different research fields almost. In ISD though, one of the major issues is to make judgements on the overall question of what kind of system to develop, i.e. to answer the question 'what is the basic purpose of the system?'. Since research treats these as separate fields, there are few attempts to develop knowledge on how to make these more general judgements, and how to choose the development method and approach appropriately.

8.2.2 System Complexity

Information systems are always complex—indeed, it is scarcely possible to imagine how a system which at its core is premised around the most elementary binary states of 1 and 0 could be composed into the incredibly complex, society transforming constructions that have ensued. An information system is a highly technical combination of computers, peripherals and software. But the complexity is not only technical. Since a system is always situated within a social context, the overall system is one of virtually infinite complexity. Still there are differences in what constitutes complexity when systems are compared. To have an understanding of complexity is something that can help in the development process. Since information systems can be regarded as complex in a number of ways, we will only discuss some aspects here.

As with almost all things in the world there is a complexity based on *size*. The larger the system, the more complex it is in every possible way. The size of an information system, with regard to number of users, number of computers and networks, is not only a question of quantity. Changes in quantity will, at certain stages, transform into qualitative differences. It is radically different to develop a system that deals with employees in an organisation of 50 employees in comparison to an organisation that has 50,000 employees. The challenges faced in the development process are drastically different and have a real impact on how to approach the development process.

An information system can be based on a technical solution ranging from a simple well-known configuration of standard components to an advanced and unique solution. The technical complexity is not necessarily dependent on the size of the system. Even a system with straightforward functionality can depend on highly specialised and complex technical designs. For instance, a large administrative database system dealing with accounting is today usually based on technical solutions that are built on standard components, both hardware and software. On the other hand, a medical system measuring body reactions, might be an extremely complex system even if developed for only a single user.

Interaction or use complexity, is another aspect of complexity that is a challenge in certain system development situations. Designing systems that are user-friendly and seduce users into using and learning more about them is at present recognised to be one of the most complex challenges in information systems development. A large number of all systems developed are dependent on the engagement of the users, of people wanting to make the system work in the intended way. Interaction complexity can differ a lot, from routine administration systems with a very simple interaction, to highly diverse systems with advanced forms of interaction, such as complex educational systems or systems based on advanced interaction technology, such as multimedia or virtual reality.

Every system is situated in some kind of context which will have impact on both people and systems. An information system changes reality, which, of course, is the purpose. This means that all information systems have ethical implications and must be understood as an active component in a larger ethical context. The way a system interacts and influences its surroundings can be seen as more or less ethically challenging. A system that inspects all email to and from an organisation, depending on its design, might be seen as extremely challenging or not from an ethical perspective. To be designed for surveillance of an individual's communication, for example, is very different to being designed as a tool to operate and optimise communication speed and reliability.

These different ways of understanding system complexity are of course not a complete list. Aspects of complexity are manifold. The point here is not to further develop all these aspects, instead we are making the case that in information systems development, the character of the system to be developed highly influences the way the development process can or must be performed. The way the complexity of the system is understood is a choice. A system with high complexity of a certain kind probably demands specific skills and competencies from the developers. The type of complexity also influences what methods to use and how to enact them as methods-in-action in the specific context.

Systems thinking is a core activity in all kinds of ISD. No matter what kind of system is being developed—the software, the organisation, the users, all taken together and situated within a larger system—demand skilled systems thinking. Besides those methods concerned specifically with ISD, there has been a long history of theories and methods developed with the purpose of facilitating systems thinking. These different systems approaches, though sometimes with radically different basic assumptions, can be a good starting point for anyone who searches for more general ways to approach complexity.

8.2.3   Solved versus Unsolved

Some systems are traditionally called 'bread and butter' systems. This is a label for a category of systems that are very common and have been developed repeatedly for many years, and as a result represent to some degree a routine solved problem. In earlier years, all systems had to be approached as if the task of the system were not solved. Even for the simplest system, no one had ever developed anything like it before. However, today most organisations use a number of systems that fall into the solved problem category. These are systems that take care of typical administrative tasks, such as payroll, accounting, or invoices. Other examples of typical solved problems are databases. Even if a database is complex in itself, the way to handle it is simplified by the use of modern database management systems (DBMS). Nowadays, systems dealing with solved problems can usually be bought as packaged software.

In contrast, unsolved problems represent a class of system that has not been developed before. This might be due to the use of new technology, or an attempt to move into a new business paradigm. Leading-edge development, focused on previously unsolved problems, has always existed. It seems as if there is a temptation to reach for new solutions, and that there are always individuals and organisations taking on the challenge and the risk. For example, the SAGE missile systems in the 1950s, the SABRE airline reservation system in the 1960s, decision support systems in the 1970s, executive information systems in the 1980s, systems to support new mould-breaking companies such as Amazon in the 1990s, and perhaps open source software solutions at the start of the new millennium. All these are examples where such attempts have been made, sometimes very successfully, sometimes not. The risk of entering new areas, where there is no conceptual understanding of what characterises that specific type of information system is high. At the same time it can be enormously rewarding. When an earlier unsolved problem is solved, a new standard is set and the space of possible information systems to develop is increased. When the spreadsheet application was first introduced, it paved the way for a completely new way of using personal computers that over time spread to larger systems.

Closely related to the aspect of solved versus unsolved problem is the issue of new versus old technology. New technology opens up new possibilities but at the same time creates new unsolved problems. Old technology is usually 'old' simply by virtue of the fact that it has survived as a technology. This means that it has proven to be reliable and to lead to the intended outcome without unpleasant unintended consequences. With new technology this is not the case. Even the simplest use of new technology is a challenge which might lead to unintended problems. To know when to take on the challenge of an unsolved problem and when to aim for a more traditional and safe solution is a fundamental aspect of ISD.

Information systems development is always part of a strategic policy, even if it is not always espoused. Choices as to what kind of technology to use and how to approach the design of that technology influence the development process.

8.2.4   Unique versus Standard

Even if we discuss families of systems here, there are still differences between systems that can be seen as generic or standard and those that are truly unique. To some extent all systems are unique since they are situated in different contexts. The total socio-technical system is therefore always unique. But, at the same time it is always possible to ignore the uniqueness and to have the context adapt to a standard system.

In the early days all information systems were unique. There was no such thing as a standard system. Today the situation is radically different. Most systems are not developed for a specific and unique context, but are standard pre-packaged software, developed with the intention of being generic so as to fit most contexts. Standard systems can today be found in all sizes and for all types of use. With regard to numbers, standard systems are most frequent within families of systems such as software for personal use, like games and personal productivity software (word-processors, databases, email software etc.). But standard systems have spread to most industries and are used in almost every type of context.

This trend has to a large extent changed the focus within ISD. Moving away from a situation where the focus was on the development of a unique IS—from requirements analysis to the very realisation of the software, with programming as the core activity, today ISD is often more a process of composition. The difficulty of creating a socio-technical system comprising both a technical and a social system is still present, but the core activity is not the production of software, instead it is the composition of the total system through evaluating, choosing, adapting, and implementing the 'right' system for the specific context, and making appropriate changes to the context.

Even if standard systems have reduced the complexity of the production of a system, it has not by any means reduced the complexity of ISD. The complexity of the development process as described in our framework is still there and has to be dealt with in every specific situation.

8.3   SYSTEMS AND CHANGE

Most information systems are developed through a process of change with the intention of reaching a stable state. The idea is that once they are finalised and implemented, systems are supposed to work and be used over time in the intended way. Studies have shown that this is not always the case. The finalised system is not something that once developed operates in the same way for the remainder of its working life. The system keeps changing over time. This has important consequences for the development process. In the design of a system the developer has to consider in what ways the system might change in the future. The developer has to consider if some changes should intentionally be supported in the design of the system, i.e. whether the systems should be designed for continuous change. Another option is to develop the system to be resistant to any change when implemented and used.

The notion that systems to a large extent do change while being used is described by Ciborra (1995) as the shifting and drifting of a system. When systems are used, people working with the system are innovative. Users come up with new unintended uses by using functions in the system in ways not designed. When this is done over time, these new use patterns are spread across the organisation and more and more users adopt the new use. This may lead to a situation where a system is effectively re-designed over time.

In the development process, a decision has to be made in regard to change. Any system can be developed to support change in use situations or to prohibit such changes. When it comes to a safety-critical system, for instance, the notion of shifting and drifting might be a cause for concern, and the system should be developed accordingly. When it comes to open and flexible solutions to support more creative use, the opposite, i.e. a system open and receptive to change, might be a better choice.

8.4   CHAPTER SUMMARY

In our discussion of the framework, we have stated that the involved parts all influence each other. This means that even the outcome of the development process, i.e. the information system, in any specific situation influences the whole framework. When the development process commences, almost everything is open and undecided. The developers have to decide how to approach the development process, how to work, what methods to use, etc. All this must be done in relation to what is imagined as the final outcome.

It is obvious that nowadays the information processing systems being developed are not all alike. As discussed above, a number of *families of systems* can be identified. In this chapter we have discussed how families of systems can be typified, for instance, by dimensions such as the purpose of the system or the complexity of the system. These different dimensions can be used to form a more general understanding of a system, even if it has to fit a unique context. The development of a unique, highly complex system for education focused on an earlier unsolved problem in the educational domain is very different from the development of a general, not so complex, administrative system focused on a standard solved problem.

This means that the way the resulting system is initially perceived has an impact on the overall framework. If the system is thought to be a highly unique, technically advanced system designed to increase efficiency in a safety critical context, the development process has to be chosen accordingly. If the purpose is to explore how an information system can be used to increase group work in a work place characterised by creative and free working conditions, a completely different approach should be chosen.

The understanding of information systems properties and types is therefore crucial, as the differing characteristics of each family serves to affect the method-in-action that will be needed to develop them.

8.5   DISCUSSION QUESTIONS

1.   Choose an information system that you frequently use and analyse it based on the discussion on "families of systems" presented in the chapter.
2.   What would be the best strategy for a developer to choose as a way to reach a deep understanding of different forms and types of information systems?
3.   Changes that might affect the design of a system will occur during ISD, as well as after implementation, i.e., when the system is being used. Discuss strategies for handling change, their possibilities and their shortcomings, both in the development phase, and when the system is being used.
4.   Looking at the "families of systems", can you see any trends that might tell us more about the future of ISD?
5.   To what extent will technology be the driving force for new types of information systems and to what extent will it be the creative and innovative skills of developers? And what does that tell us about the future?

9

The Framework-in-Action: Method Tailoring

9.1 INTRODUCTION

Despite the fact that formalised ISD methods are scrupulously documented, prescribing in minute detail the exact sequence of steps to be followed, our research has revealed that in practice developers rarely follow the sequence of steps as prescribed in the method. As a consequence, newer versions of existing methods now almost routinely recommend some contingent *tailoring*. Notwithstanding this, there is very little by way of practical guidance to inform developers as to what steps to modify or omit. Much is left to the intuition of individual developers. This is understandable, but ensures that all tailoring efforts are undertaken in an ad hoc fashion with little transfer of learning between projects.

This chapter attempts to contribute to an increased understanding of the tailoring issue. The approach taken is slightly different from the conventional one, in which we might identify some principles and tenets for method tailoring which had been derived deductively from some *a priori* stated set of axioms in the existing literature as to how method tailoring might take place. Rather, we focus in-depth here on method tailoring in a very formalised development environment in a particular high-profile software development organisation, a very large multi-national telecommunications company. From this case, we draw lessons on tailoring which should be applicable to other organisations worldwide. Even if an organisation decides that this level of tailoring is not feasible or appropriate for the development context, the case does provide a useful basis for discussion of the tailoring issue.

However, we begin by sketching out a brief background of previous research relevant to method tailoring.

9.2   PREVIOUS RESEARCH RELEVANT TO METHOD TAILORING

Little research appears to have been conducted on the specific topic of method tailoring. However, two closely-related areas are *contingency factors research* and *method engineering*. These are briefly summarised here and their relationship to method tailoring discussed.

9.2.1   Contingency Factors Research

Contingency factors in ISD methods have been the subject of much ISD research in the past (e.g. Avison & Wood-Harper, 1991; Benyon & Skidmore, 1987; Davis, 1982; Gremillion & Pyburn, 1983; Iivari, 1989; Shomenta *et al.*, 1983). Contingency research is typically premised on the notion that specific features of the development context are mapped to the selection of an appropriate ISD method from a portfolio of methods.

Davis (1982) represents an early and widely cited contribution. He considered the area of information requirements determination and evaluated alternative strategies for this. He proposed a contingency approach based on an assessment of different levels of uncertainty in the overall development context through which an appropriate strategy would be selected from among several available alternatives. Thus, in Davis' model, an organisation would be expected to have a range of methods available to developers, who would presumably be fully *au fait* with each method, and the most appropriate one would then be chosen depending on the contingencies of the situation.

In a similar fashion, Gremillion & Pyburn (1983) also recommended a contingency approach proposing that development projects be evaluated according to the criteria of commonality, impact and structure before deciding on a development approach, which could range from the traditional approach, prototyping, or an application package solution.

Iivari (1989) has argued for a pragmatic contingency approach and provided a framework which illustrated how certain methods had been incorporating a contingency approach. However, his approach differed from that of Davis (1982) in that he argued for built-in contingency as a feature of the method itself. Thus, he was not arguing for a repertoire of methods; rather, the encompassing framework of the method was expected to cover all situations.

Avison & Wood-Harper (1991) reviewed various ISD methods and concluded that none could be appropriate in all situations. Adhering more to the Iivari model than that of Davis, they proposed their favoured method, Multiview, as a contingency framework which could incorporate the tools and techniques relevant to a particular context. They also acknowledged the difficulties that could arise in using a contingency approach. Multiview has since evolved into Multiview 2, which takes the contingency approach to an advanced level, in which the situation-specific method is derived through multi-perspective reflection on the role of the analyst (and other stake-holders), the problem context and the particular methodological support required (Avison *et al.*, 1998).

A similar approach which was proposed by Benyon & Skidmore (1987) was to create a single "tool kit" which combined the essential features of a range of methods which they suggested were complementary. The methods proposed included soft systems methodology, the structured approach, the data-centred approach, and the participative approach (these have been discussed in Chapters 3 and 4 above). The expectation was that developers would be skilled enough to choose the appropriate method or tool depending on the situation. While the different methods proposed are indeed complementary, ranging from 'soft' to 'hard', and from process-driven to data-driven, the tool-kit approach has been criticised as being inadequate (Avison *et al.*, 1988).

Shomenta *et al.*, (1983) developed their Application Approach Worksheet as a tool which could be used to help developers and users make the transition from using one development approach to using a variety of tools and approaches. Based on various characteristics of an application, the worksheet guided the selection of approach, either traditional, end-user computing via a 4GL on the mainframe, or end-user development using a microcomputer-based package.

9.2.2   Method Engineering Research

The contingency approach in general has been the subject of criticism by Kumar & Welke (1992). Their contention was that existing methods did not adequately cover all contingencies, and further, that the cost of sourcing and training for each method that was required by the contingencies of development would be prohibitive. This situation would be further exacerbated by the rapid and fundamental changes in the prevailing development environment in organisations. In addition to this, the contingency litera-ture contained little by way of practical guidelines as to how methods or tools could be mapped to development contingencies. The solution proposed by Kumar & Welke was that of method engineering.

Harmesen *et al.* (1994) have traced the origins of the concept of method engineering to mechanical engineering in the 1930s (Maynard & Stegemerten, 1939). They acknowledge the advantage of ISD methods in their provision of a disciplined standard for development, but recognise that flexibility is necessary in order that methods be 'tuned' to meet specific project needs. Their objective has been the "harmonisation of methods" through the provision of a strategy for constructing situational methods out of existing proven method fragments. To operationalise this they have suggested a method base repository which would contain suitable method fragments. Harmesen *et al.* provide quite a detailed description of the application of situational method engineering; however, the case they use to illustrate their approach is drawn from a literature example (Olle, 1988) rather than real-life practice. As discussed in Chapter 5, the failure to validate ISD approaches in real-life development practice is all too common.

Kumar & Welke (1992) argued that design methods must themselves be designed, and proposed a recursive step whereby the method would itself be designed using a meta-method. They suggested that methods be represented as discrete pre-defined and pre-tested components. These could then be drawn upon to construct a method quickly, cheaply and efficiently. They identified a number of strategies which would need to be accommodated in such a meta-method. The component base should be based on stakeholder values and supported by automated computer-based support as well as the organisational structure. The automated support should allow for seamless integration of the modular components. Tutorials and training aids should also be part of the package.

This recursivity feature of method engineering is similar to an older argument about programming languages (Tolvanen, 1998). In research on method engineering, Tolvanen proposed the use of metamodelling, suggesting that a metamodel be used to capture information about the concepts, representation forms, and uses of a method. Metamodels are divided into two categories, meta-data models which describe the static aspects of a method, and meta-process models which describe the dynamics of a method. Tolvanen has argued that metamodelling provides advantages in terms of representing, systematising and comparing methods. He argued that many methods were defined quite vaguely, and suggested that method users, already familiar with modelling techniques, would be very competent at analysing methods which have been metamodelled. This metamodelling approach has been implemented in a commercially available configurable CASE tool, MetaEdit.

One marked feature of both the contingency and method engineering research is that they are largely deductive in nature as they employ theoretical and conceptual arguments to support how methods should be tailored or constructed. Very little is available in terms of practical applications of these ideas in real life. We try to bridge this gap here by grounding this section on method tailoring in the actual practice of ISD in an organisation.

9.3   THE METHOD TAILORING FRAMEWORK

Fig. 9.1 depicts the nature of the method tailoring in the particular organisation. Again, as in previous sections, the individual components of the framework are explained in more detail below.

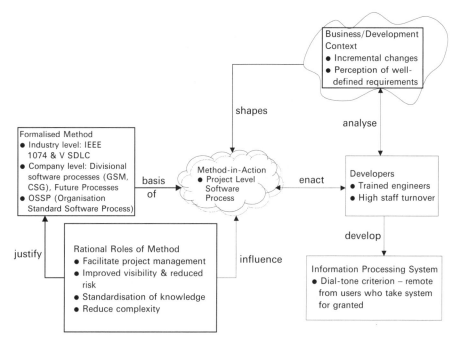

Fig. 9.1   Method Tailoring-in-Action at Telco

9.3.1   Information Processing Systems

Telco is a major systems provider in the mobile telecommunications sector. These systems are very large and expensive switching and communications infrastructure systems. The nature of the environment in which these systems operate is one in which users (individuals who make telephone calls) take the underlying system completely for granted and expect total reliability—the so-called 'dial tone' criterion. That is, customers take for granted the fact that they will always hear a dial-tone when they pick up a traditional land-line telephone. Given the fact that there are several very significant and reputable competitors in the marketplace, the reliability of the Telco systems is very important. Also, the telecommunications technology area is one that is constantly evolving, with new products and services continually on offer. Thus, systems are constantly being adapted to incorporate interfaces to these new developments. The systems themselves are developed using common languages such as C and C++.

9.3.2   Development Context

Large teams of developers work on each project and the development environment is very formalised. The development process is also very formalised. The organisation has explicitly documented their fundamental software process, the Organisational Standard Software Process (OSSP). This is tailored precisely to the development process for each project and is then followed rigorously on all projects. It is evolving as the company follows their programme for continuous process improvement, which will ultimately lead to an improved rating on the Capability Maturity Model (CMM) (Paulk *et al.*, 1993). A large amount of metric data on the development process is collected and analysed, and this information is later displayed on notice boards for the attention of developers.

The strong technical and engineering nature of the environment is evident in the belief that requirements that can be well-defined in advance. However, this is facilitated by the fact that the majority of development represents fairly incremental functional changes to existing systems—making new features available, for example. Thus, the broad characteristics of the projects can be defined *a priori*. Again, this is represented in Fig. 9.1 by a rectangle superimposed on the development context to reflect the fact that the untidy messy nature of requirements analysis is not a feature of this development context.

9.3.3   Developers

Telco have over 400 engineers working on systems development in their European headquarters in Ireland. Developers tend to have a very strong technical background in engineering or computer science. Clients are typically very large telecommunications providers who purchase Telco systems to support their telephone network infrastructures. New employees are made aware of the OSSP via induction training sessions. Satisfying the concepts of the CMM is very important to Telco, and a specialist group—the Process Engineering Group—exists within the company to ensure that the CMM criteria are complied with. Such an environment feels very constraining to some developers who desire more autonomy and discretion in their work. Thus, they leave to seek a less formalised development environment in some other organisation.

9.3.4   Formalised Method Tailoring

Telco perform some macro-level tailoring to arrive at the overall standard ISD method at the organisational level, the Organisational Standard Software Process (OSSP), as mentioned above. This then becomes the basis for micro-level tailoring of the method for each individual project, which will be discussed in the method-in-action section below.

Macro-Level Method Tailoring at the Industry Level

The highest level at which Telco begin the tailoring process is what we term the Industry level. We have chosen the label 'industry level' because the components used here are available more or less universally to any organisation developing software in that they are part of the public domain. Here, the two basic elements on which Telco ground their development method are the IEEE 1074 software standard (IEEE, 1991) and the V software lifecycle model (V-SLCM) (cf. Sommerville, 1992). The IEEE 1074 standard is a very detailed one which prescribes a very detailed set of essential activities that are seen as mandatory for the development and maintenance of software. Telco perceive a number of significant benefits in adopting the IEEE 1074 standard. Firstly, it represents an internationally-recognised standard for development which is evolving, but in a controlled and rigorous manner. Also, the standard is complementary to the CMM, which is very important in Telco as a means of assessing the maturity of their development process and also as a mechanism to introduce improvements to that process.

While the IEEE 1074 standard is detailed and comprehensive, it is recognised that it will need to be tailored in context. The standard explicitly specifies that an actual software development lifecycle (SDLC) model be chosen, to which the activities can be mapped. The SDLC concept was discussed earlier in Chapter 3. A number of SDLC models exist, including the Waterfall (Royce, 1970), the Spiral (Boehm, 1988), and the V-model (Sommerville, 1992). The latter has been chosen by Telco to complement the IEEE 1074 standard. However, by constructing their ISD method from discrete components, Telco could introduce an alternative lifecycle model if they wished; indeed, the Spiral model is currently being investigated by Telco. Also, the IEEE 1074 standard merely prescribes the *processes* for the lifecycle. The *products* of the lifecycle in terms of specific documents and deliverables must subsequently be mapped to the method. Thus, tailoring is very much an inherent requirement of the IEEE 1074 standard.

Macro-Level Method Tailoring at the Organisational Level

At the organisational level, a number of software processes exist which are specific to the various parent divisions within Telco and naturally they influence the process in the Irish operation. These divisions include the GPD (GSM Product Division) and the CSG (Cellular Switching Group), which are both US-based. Each of these divisions has configured their software process to suit the exigencies of their particular development environment. For example, sub-contractor management is relevant to the GPD division but not to the other. Also, Telco found that some of their common software processes were not covered in sufficient depth by the IEEE 1074 standard, testing and software maintenance issues being two examples. Thus, these needed to be factored into the organisational development process.

Finally, at the organisational level, it is recognised that some development projects in the future might require processes which are not accommodated by the current method. One possible example might be that a customer would seek some intermediate delivery of a product after design and prior to system testing. This would require a change to the existing processes. Thus, the existence of the Future Project Processes component ensures flexibility to cater for the contingencies that may arise in future development scenarios.

Based on these considerations, the overall Organisational Standard Software Process (OSSP) is constructed. As can be seen from the discussion above, the process is already characterised by a good deal of tailoring. However, the tailoring is at a macro-level in that the specifics of the individual projects have not yet been factored in. At the organisational level, the main emphasis is on creating a trusted, rigorous and reliable software process which has already absorbed the sequencing aspects of a software lifecycle model (in this case, the V model). Also, the CMM key process areas (see Chapter 3) are explicitly factored into the method at this level.

The OSSP is reasonably stable although it is expected to evolve, and, indeed, the capability to evolve is built into the model. It represents the general process that each project is expected to follow, being the operational definition of the fundamental process elements and their inter-relationships. This strategy overcomes a problem identified with both method engineering and contingency approaches, namely, that organisations in practice clearly cannot afford to wait while a lengthy tailoring process takes place. In the Telco case, much of the broad macro-level tailoring is done in advance to create a formalised method that may be the basis of micro-level tailoring to create the method-in-action at the individual project level.

9.3.5   Project Level Tailoring: Method-in-Action

Following the construction of the OSSP, a phase of micro-level tailoring of the method takes place at the level of individual projects. This is where the project-specific characteristics are factored in. In essence, certain elements of the OSSP are chosen depending on the operational needs of the project. Since the OSSP process elements cover all aspects of the software process including those practices which are project specific; e.g. sub-contractor management or project planning, and those practices which are non-project specific, e.g. training or process improvement, the project specific elements of the OSSP must be selected to address the operational needs of the project. The project manager is responsible for this level of tailoring. Following this, specific characteristics or features of the actual project under development are considered and further refinements to the project lifecycle are duly made. Some of these tailoring decisions will be made at the start of the project and recorded in the project plan. For example, it may be decided to produce a High Level and a Low Level Design specification, as opposed to a simpler Detailed Design specification, for a particular software feature if that feature is judged to be particularly complex. Other tailoring decisions will be made dynamically in the course of the project. For example, if commitments change significantly after a project has started, then, based on an impact assessment of the change, it may be decided to invoke the Project Re-Planning process or absorb the impact in the current schedule.

Tailoring at this level also applies to areas that are non-project specific. For example a change to the test process may or may not require piloting based on an impact assessment of the process change. Another example might be to grant a developer a waiver from a particular training course if they satisfy certain criteria.

9.3.6   Roles of Method

The roles of method that are emphasised in Telco are the rational intellectual ones that were discussed in some detail in Chapter 5 earlier. The necessity to manage projects carefully in the highly competitive market-place is paramount. Also, because the system must satisfy the 'dial-tone' level of reliability, the necessity for a rigorous development process is seen as paramount. It is vital that errors and downtime are kept to a minimum. When errors do occur in systems, a very precise process for handling the situation is mandated. All fixes undergo rigorous testing before they are released to the customer. Thus, risk of regression errors is minimised.

It is a very formalised development environment, and Telco maintain a vast amount of metric data on the outcome of development projects. Thus, they are constantly trying to capture knowledge from past projects. The OSSP represents an attempt to capture the high level lessons that have been learned and formally captured in the divisional software processes. This method is then taught as part of the induction process for new employees.

9.4   CHAPTER SUMMARY

This chapter has drawn upon our framework to analyse method tailoring in a large multi-national telecommunications company. A very sophisticated dual level method tailoring process has been institutionalised within the company. Firstly, an initial macro level of tailoring is undertaken to produce a standard development method for general use. This has resulted in a robust formalised method which incorporates the lessons learned from ISD in the organisation in the past—the Organisation Standard Software Process (OSSP). This then forms the basis for subsequent micro level tailoring of the process for each individual project. Such a level of tailoring seems to be necessary in practice, but most organisations fail to adopt such a strategy. Many organisations now realise the futility of trying to adopt a formalised method in the strictly prescribed sequence that is suggested in the accompanying manuals and textbooks.

In the past, method tailoring initiatives in most organisations have been quite ad hoc, and much has been left to the intuition of individual developers. However, even where organisations have formally undertaken some method tailoring, these tailoring approaches tend to fall into two groups, both of which are fundamentally flawed. Firstly, they may attempt to begin the entire tailoring effort from scratch with their chosen method every time, rather than creating an intermediate method which has already been broadly tailored to the context in the first place (the OSSP in the case described above), and which can then be used as a starting point for subsequent tailoring on each project. Alternatively, many organisations perform a once-off tailoring of their chosen method, and then mandate that this tailored method be used in all development situations without any subsequent micro-level fine-tuning. Neither of these approaches is adequate clearly.

As ISD theory and practice becomes increasingly mature, tailoring is going to become a more pressing topic, and the approach identified in this chapter has much to recommend it, given its foundation in a complex development context in practice.

9.5   DISCUSSION QUESTIONS

1.   Given the necessity for method tailoring, why do you think there has been so little academic research or practitioner advice on the issue?

2.   In what types of organisation or development context is the method tailoring approach, discussed here, appropriate? In what types of organisation or development context would this approach not be appropriate?

3.   How suited is the method engineering approach to ISD in general? Are there additional advantages or disadvantages to method tailoring other than those suggested here?

4.   What competencies or skills are needed by developers when method tailoring is chosen?

5.   Method tailoring is, as discussed in the chapter, something that can be approached in a methodical manner. It might even be possible to have a method for choosing a method that helps you tailor a method to a specific development context. Is there a problem of levels involved here? How can this be dealt with?

10

The Framework-in-Action: New Directions in ISD

10.1 INTRODUCTION

The framework presented in this book is meant to be general and inclusive. Our intention is that it be used as a tool for analysing and understanding different forms of ISD practice. We believe that this becomes more and more important since the field of ISD is constantly changing. While earlier systems development was a fairly structured and recognisable process in many settings, today this traditional understanding of ISD is challenged by rapidly changing preconditions.

This chapter draws on our framework to illustrate the nature of ISD practice in a number of current development scenarios. The scenarios discussed here include *open source software development*, *ERP development*, and *web development*. These three scenarios should not be seen as an inclusive list of current practices. Instead they are chosen because they represent new forms of practices that to many practitioners are part of their everyday experience, at the same time as they challenge our common and traditional understanding of ISD.

The presentation of the scenarios fulfils two purposes. Firstly, it is a way to show how the framework can be used to structure the analysis and understanding of a specific form of ISD without having to go into all the details of the complexity of each new approach. The unique aspects of these scenarios can be depicted using the framework. Secondly, these scenarios provide a means to test the framework itself. One major argument in this book is that ISD is at the core of the information systems field, even if new paradigms and new approaches claim to change the very basis for

ISD. We argue that the analysis presented in this chapter illustrates the strength of the framework and its general applicability. We also believe that this shows how the framework can serve as a tool for analysis and evaluation of new approaches.

Each of the chosen scenarios is described and analysed by relating them to the framework. The purpose is to see in what way ISD is present and in what form it appears when it is challenged by new practices. It can be understood as the "framework-in-action".

10.2   THE FRAMEWORK-IN-ACTION: OPEN SOURCE SOFTWARE DEVELOPMENT

As already mentioned in Chapter 4, a detailed treatment of the OSS phenomenon is beyond the scope of this book (a detailed discussion of the OSS phenomenon is provided in Feller & Fitzgerald, 2002). However, briefly summarising, open source software is software in which the distribution should include the source code (or it should be downloadable at no cost), the code should be modifiable, and the code should be re-distributable without conditions by third-parties.

It should be evident from this book thus far that software development is a problematic area, so much so that the term 'software crisis' was coined to reflect this back in 1968. Simply summarising the software crisis refers to the fact that software costs too much to develop, takes too long to develop, and is not of very high quality when eventually delivered.

While the definition of open source software above might seem to address only the cost aspect of the software crisis, the development process that has arisen in open source software seems to be very radical, and to address all the other aspects of the software crisis. In terms of speed of development, for example, the Linux operating system and other OSS products mentioned in Chapter 4 are characterised by a very rapid development time-scale, with new releases of Linux being produced more than once per day in the early days of its development. The third aspect of the software crisis, software quality, is also addressed by the OSS approach, in that OSS developers are reckoned to be the most talented and highly motivated 5 per cent of software developers (Raymond, 2001). Also, peer review of any development product is truly independent in OSS development, in that the global community of co-developers have no vested interest, consciously or subconsciously, in turning a blind eye to deficiencies in the product. Evidence of this quality and inherent reliability of OSS output is amply demonstrated by the fact that these products have achieved such a significant market share without any conventional marketing or advertising campaigns.

We have summarised the OSS development process using our framework in Fig. 10.1. The individual components of the framework are discussed in subsequent sections.

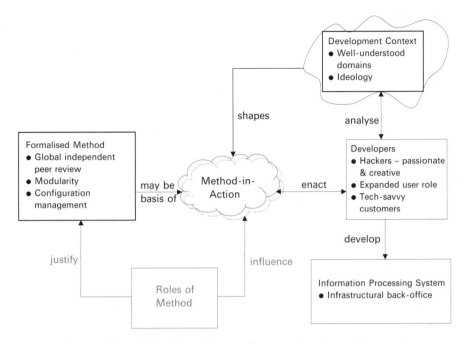

Fig. 10.1   Open Source Software Development

10.2.1 OSS Development Context

OSS products tend to be of the technical, infrastructural type—operating systems, system utilities, and networking technologies. OSS software appears to be best suited to horizontal domains where design is almost a given. That is there is widespread agreement on design architecture, and the general shape of the software requirements is fairly well known and not problematic. This is probably essential if contributions are to be drawn from developers with a wide variety of industry backgrounds and also from students and researchers in academe. There is no real scope in the process for an extensive discussion of requirements analysis or design decisions. These must be generally agreed upon if literally thousands of developers are to work towards some commonly recognised goal. On the other hand, in vertical domains where requirements and design issues are a function of specific domain knowledge that can only really be acquired over time—the case in many business environments, in fact—then there are not likely to be many OSS offerings. This simplification of the requirements definition and design process is depicted in Fig. 10.1 as a rectangle superimposed on the development context. This is intended to reflect the fact that requirements analysis is taken as given and universally agreed upon, rather than being the unpredictable, negotiated aspect that it is in most business contexts.

10.2.2 OSS Developers

A common myth is that OSS developers are teenage hackers operating from their bedrooms. While not much is really known about the exact nature of the OSS development community, the notion of OSS developers being solely teenage hacker is a mythical stereotype. Different estimates have been made as to the size of the OSS development community. Markus *et al.* (2000) estimate the total community of OSS developers to number 750,000, whereas OSS evangelists claim the Linux development community alone comprises that figure (Raymond, 2001; Torvalds & Diamond, 2001). More detailed studies reveal that developers tend to come in equal proportions from both the US and Europe; thus, the US bias that exists in IT in general does not appear to be reproduced in OSS development. Also, it appears that many OSS contributors are actual professional developers working in traditional software companies (cf. Feller and Fitzgerald, 2002).

OSS developers are often motivated to develop the software initially by a need for a product which they cannot easily acquire from any other source—"scratching a personal itch" to use Raymond's (2001) memorable term. This is another reason why requirements analysis tends to be seen as unproblematic, in that the first conception of the system is for personal needs and a formal requirements analysis process would not then be seen as necessary. These developers tend to be technically very gifted, and the initial software they produce is enthusiastically received by their peers. Also, these developers tend to be very passionate about the work they do, and this seems to be contagious. Other developers seek the validation of positive feedback from these initial pioneers. Thus, a strong sense of community is built up over time, and the positive feelings of community belonging are an important source of motivation for individual OSS developers.

Ideology also plays an important part for OSS developers, whether it be to challenge Microsoft's or the US dominance in software, or to span the digital divide between the West and developing countries.

In addition, OSS elaborates the role that non-technical users can play in development. For example, they may provide feedback to help elaborate requirements. Also, they can help in system testing, or in developing documentation, all tasks that developers are often fairly reluctant to undertake.

10.2.3 OSS Systems

Most of the OSS products that have emerged to date have been general-purpose, horizontal infrastructure software—operating systems, utilities, networking technologies, and the like. An interesting exception to this, however, is the case of databases. These fall into the horizontal general-purpose software category. They may be complex software, but are no more so than an operating system, for example. However, there are no real commercial OSS databases—products such as MySQL, and BerkeleyDB exist but they do not compete in this arena. The most likely explanation is that databases have not appeared in the "personal itches" of any OSS developers thus far.

Of significance is the fact that OSS is the choice of the technologically literate user/customers. These customers would not be swayed by any slick marketing campaign, and in fact would probably view that as a waste of money. They are aware of the advantages of OSS products, and are willing to tolerate the absence of niceties such as a user-friendly interface. This phenomenon would appear to be borne out in the comments of a user who installed Linux and then posted a message on a network referring to the "thrilling adventure" of that installation (cf. Feller & Fitzgerald, 2002).

10.2.4   OSS Development: Formalised Method to Method-in-Action

Part of the conventional wisdom of software development is captured in Brooks' fundamental law which states that "adding manpower to a late software project makes it later" (Brooks, 1975). Based on this, it was thought that complex software required a disciplined and orderly approach, and that the communication overhead of adding extra developers negated their potential contribution to development productivity. This leads to the belief that due to the inherent complexity of software, it should be developed using tightly co-ordinated, centralised teams, following a rigorous development process. Raymond (2001) categorised this mode of development as a *cathedral*-style. He contrasted this with a *bazaar*-style of development, which better characterised the open source development approach.

The bazaar metaphor was chosen to reflect the babbling, apparent confusion of a middle-Eastern marketplace. In terms of software development, this style does not mandate any particular development approach—all are free to develop in their own way and to follow their own agenda. There is no formal procedure to ensure that developers are not duplicating effort by working on the same problem. In conventional software development, such duplication of effort would be seen as wasteful, but in the open source bazaar model, it leads to a greater exploration of the problem space, and is consistent with an evolutionary principle of mutation and survival of the fittest, in so far as the best solution is likely to be incorporated into the evolving software product (Kuwabara, 2000). Certainly, the bazaar model would appear to be capable of astonishing results. For example, Linux was begun five years after Microsoft Windows NT, with no budget and relying on voluntary contributions; yet, as already mentioned, new releases of the Linux kernel were being released more than once per day at one stage. Thus, the OSS community have recast Brooks' Law as "given enough eye-balls, every bug looks shallow" (Raymond, 2001) to reflect the manner in which the literally global community of OSS co-developers, operating in a decentralised co-operative manner according to the principle of prompt feedback, are able to solve the various problems that arise. Linux has had more than 1000 developers working on the kernel alone, while Fetchmail has had more than 600 globally-distributed co-developers working asynchronously in different time-zones (Raymond, 2001).

This provides further support for OSS as a silver bullet—feedback is very prompt, the testing pool is global, peer review is truly independent, the contributors are in the top 5 per cent of developers world-wide in terms of ability, and they are self-selected and highly motivated. However, the truly amazing aspect of OSS is that this 'silver bullet' arises from a process which at first glance appears to be completely alien to the fundamental tenets and conventional wisdom of software engineering, i.e. it appears as if the method is anarchistic. For example, in the bazaar development style, there is no real formal design process, there is no risk assessment nor measurable goals, no direct monetary incentives for developers or organisations, informal co-ordination and control, much duplication in parallel effort. All of these are anathema to conventional software engineering.

However, 30 years of ISD research cannot be easily discounted. Thus, an examination of the details of the OSS development process serves to question the extent to which software engineering principles are actually being fundamentally overturned. Firstly, the main contributors of the OSS community are acknowledged to be superb coders, suggested by some to be among the top 5 per cent of programmers in terms of their skills (Raymond, 2001). Also, as they are self-selected, they are highly motivated to contribute. The remarkable potential of gifted individuals has long been recognised in IS development, as discussed in Chapter 7. Brooks (1987) suggests that good programmers may be a hundred times more productive than mediocre ones. The Chief Programmer Team more than twenty years ago also bore witness to the potential of great programmers (Baker, 1972; Mills, 1971). Also, in more recent times, the capability maturity model (CMM), discussed in Chapter 4, recognises that fabulous success in software development has often been achieved due to the "heroics of talented individuals" (Paulk et al., 1993). Thus, given the widely recognised talent of the OSS leaders, the success of OSS products may not be such a complete surprise.

The advancement of knowledge in software engineering has certainly been incorporated into OSS software. Linux, for example, benefited a great deal from the evolution of Unix in that defects were eliminated and requirements fleshed out a great deal (McConnell, 1999). Furthermore, some of the fundamental concepts of software engineering in relation to cohesion and coupling and modularity of code are very much a feature of OSS. Linux, by being based on Unix, is very modular in its architecture. Indeed, the manner in which different individuals can take responsibility for different self-contained modules within Linux, is acknowledged as being a major factor in its successful evolution. Further evidence of the importance of modularity arises from the Sendmail utility. This was first developed by Eric Allmen at Berkeley in the late 70s, and the source made available to interested parties. However, as it began to evolve through the contributions of others, problems in integrating contributions began to arise. Allmen resigned from his position and rewrote the software completely to follow a more modular structure. This ensured that it could be a suitable candidate for the massive parallel development, characteristic of OSS, as developers could work largely independently on different aspects. Sendmail has evolved to its current position of dominance—estimated to route 80 per cent of all Internet mail. These examples provide much evidence that open source software does obey the fundamental tenets of software engineering in relation to modularity.

Configuration management, another important research area within software engineering, is a vitally important factor within OSS, and is typically catered for by the Concurrent Versioning System (CVS), a product which is itself OSS. Also, the software engineering principles of independent peer review and testing are very highly evolved to an extremely advanced level within OSS.

The traditional software development life cycle (SDLC) is premised on a set of generic stages, which typically comprise planning, analysis, design, and implementation. However, the OSS development life cycle is very different. Firstly, the planning, analysis and design phases are largely conducted by the initial project founder, and are not part of the general OSS development life cycle. However, getting design issues right is perhaps even more critical in OSS than in conventional development. Also, design decisions are generally made in advance, before the larger pool of developers start to contribute, and are generally based on well-established design patterns. This allows developers to collaborate without having to undergo the detailed requirements analysis or design phases of the traditional life cycle. In the absence of conventional project management, the importance of "having a tail-light to follow" (Bezroukov 1999) is a very useful coordinating principle, as it allows a multitude of developers to contribute.

This also helps to explain why many OSS products are horizontal infrastructure type products, as these are ones in which the requirements are pretty well understood. In vertical domains, developer knowledge of the application domain has been found to be critical, but it is unlikely that the pool of potential developers would be as large in such domains.

In summary, then, the code in OSS products is often very structured and modular in the first place, contributions are carefully vetted and incorporated in a very disciplined fashion in accordance with good configuration management, independent peer review and testing. Thus, on closer inspection, the bazaar model of OSS does not depart wildly from many of the sensible and proven fundamental software engineering principles. The argument then that OSS begins as a bazaar with a chaotic development process chaos and evolves mysteriously into a co-ordinated process with an exceptionally high quality end-product is too simplistic a characterisation of what actually is taking place in practice.

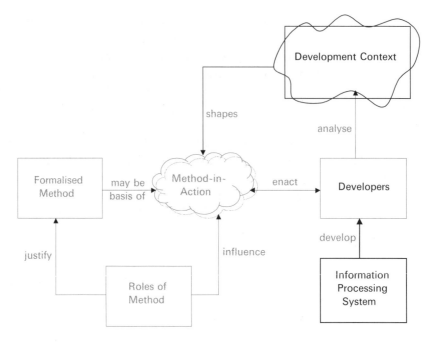

Fig. 10.2   ERP Systems Development

10.3   THE FRAMEWORK-IN-ACTION: ERP SYSTEMS

ERP systems create new challenges for ISD, as they form new relationships between the different parts of the development framework. ERP systems change the understanding of what constitutes the context and they present new demands for competence from developers. Fig. 10.2 illustrates the nature of ERP systems development. Each of the significant aspects of the framework is discussed below.

10.3.1 ERP Development Context

As discussed in Chapter 4, ERP systems development reverses the traditional sequence of the development process which moves from the analysis of a set of requirements to designing an information system to satisfy those requirements. Rather, the ERP development process implies that development proceeds on the basis of beginning with the overall functionality that the system can possibly provide and then eliminating the functions that are not necessary.

Fig. 10.2 illustrates the complex dynamic that results. For example, the rectangle in the development context represents the functionality provided by the ERP system. In Fig 10.2 we can see that some parts of the rectangle lie outside the irregular boundary which represents the actual requirements of development context. This reflects the fact that the ERP system by being designed as the highest common denominator for a vast range of organisational requirements will provide a wide range of functions some of which will not be relevant to any given particular organisation. Thus, these functions will remain unused even though paid for and available in the original system.

However, a more sinister phenomenon is the inverse situation. That is, when the idiosyncrasies of the organisational context are not satisfied by the available functionality in the ERP system. This is reflected in Fig. 10.2 in the those portions of the irregular shape of the development context which lie outside the boundaries of the rectangle. This represents those requirements peculiar to the particular organisational context which cannot be satisfied by the functionality available within the ERP system.

The role of the context changes drastically in this setting. Traditionally the context is the natural starting point of development work. The context is seen as providing a problem, and the problem is the motivation for the development from the very beginning. The context also defines what are the basic business activities that have to be supported by an information system. All this changes when an organisation turns to the use of ERP systems. Since the overlap between the system functionality and the organisational requirements (as shown in Fig. 10.2) is not a precise fit, the preconditions for the future of the context has changed. Traditionally the system to be developed is understood as the part of the totality that can be designed according to needs. Now the organisation, the context, is accorded that role. The system becomes the background based on which a 're-design' of the context must be performed.

The context is no longer the fixed background, instead the system is. This has an impact on what can be seen as the functionality of the total system. It actually forces information system development to be something much larger. ISD becomes a strategic development of the context, that is, the whole organisation. ISD defines what the organisation can do and how it can do it. ERP creates a more or less fixed background for the development of the organisation instead of the opposite. To some extent this makes the whole issue of what really constitutes the system and what constitutes the context diffuse. This has direct consequence for the developers of information systems.

10.3.2 ERP Developers

ERP systems are large and complex systems. The basic idea is that the system should cater for the whole range of needs of a large number of organisations, and as a consequence, these systems are large both in size and functionality. The usual challenge for a developer in a traditional setting is to be creative in how to interpret the needs of the organisation, and to have the ability to transform these needs into requirements leading to the specification of a suitable system. This means that ISD is a one-way approach, from context to system. In the case of ERP development, that approach changes. The developer has to start with two endpoints, the context and the system, and has to be creative in the way they can be adapted to each other. Either by changing the way the organisation carries out its activities or by configuring the system (within the limits of its functionality).

Another impact that ERP systems have on the everyday work of developers is due to the simple fact that these are large systems. When organisations use several information systems, each focused on one specific functionality or aspect of the everyday activities, a developer can have some overall understanding of a specific system, even if he or she still only works with parts of that system. In the setting of an ERP system, this is impossible. An ERP system covers so many functions within the organisation, to the extent that, even if it is only one system, the developer cannot possibly understand the whole, either on the context side, or on the system side.

For developers, this creates new challenges and new questions concerning competence. Traditionally the skill and competence of a developer could be applied in many different contexts. The skill was not focused on one specific system even if it might be around a certain type of system. The competence of an ERP developer is much closer related to the specifics of that system. The complexity of the system also creates a situation where it takes a very long time to get a deep understanding of the system. In traditional ISD, developers usually developed a competence within a specific domain or context, such as banking, government administration, process industry. With ERP that kind of deep understanding is instead focused on the specific information system.

ERP systems are sold by a small number of vendors—often described as BOPS representing Baan, Oracle, Peoplesoft and SAP respectively. However, the large consultancy companies are very much part of ERP development in that the ERP vendors recommend that knowledgeable consultants who have detailed knowledge of the vast range of system parameters be involved in development. Given the huge world-wide deployment of these systems, ERP developers are a scarce commodity who are in big demand, and attract enormous daily consultancy fees.

10.3.3 ERP Systems

ERP systems aim to provide a configurable suite of systems to satisfy an organisation's overall information processing needs. Basically, these are all-encompassing systems that may be tailored to the contingencies of different organisational requirements by configuring a broad range of parameters. Ironically, in an era when much has been made of using information systems to achieve competitive advantage, ERP systems limits the scope for this in that they homogenise information systems. That is, if all organisations are using the same ERP systems, then the scope from achieving any distinct competitive advantage from an organisation's information systems is considerably reduced.

One aspect of this can be seen in Fig. 10.2. Since the system covers areas outside the context, the way the system is designed influences in what direction the organisation can develop and grow. Even if ERP systems can be adjusted by setting parameters, the basic design is done at the generic level. The more an organisation makes changes or additions to the basic structure of the system, i.e., the more they adapt the system to their needs, the more they deviate from the generic system. This is reported as one of the most difficult judgements involved in ERP development. If the specific implementation of an ERP system is adapted too much, it drastically increases the problems and complexity when new versions of the generic system are released. There is a delicate balance between the generic system and the adapted version implemented.

The complexity of the total system creates problems of overview, and even of efficiency. One of the basic research issues concerning the use of ERP is therefore the overall efficiency. The quest for a total system for the purpose of avoiding redundancy might lead to systems that are so complex that new forms of efficiency traps appear. Small systems are usually quite easy to adjust since it is possible to see what are the consequences of every adjustment. In a large ERP system there is a possibility for unintended consequences, and in parts of the system where it is impossible to detect. The internal logic of the whole system is too complex. Whether or not the problem of complexity will create larger drawbacks than the intended benefits from having one single total system is something which is still undecided.

10.3.4 ERP Development: From Formalised Method to Method-in-Action

ERP systems impose new demands on the development process. The traditional skills involved in ISD such as the design of software structure and functions and, of course, programming, are no longer as relevant. The development process when it comes to ERP systems is different. At the same time, the need for an overall understanding of the process, such as the one we present in our framework, is still needed. Even if new competence is needed and the process is not the same, the development is still a complex process, and a process that must be guided by some kind of method or approach.

ERP systems are based on the idea of reducing the complexity of building new systems by using ready-made generic systems. As shown above this does not necessarily lead to less complexity. We believe that the introduction of ERP systems does not reduce the overall complexity in ISD (as presented in our framework), instead it shifts and moves the complexity from one part of the framework to another. There is nothing in the ERP approach that makes any part of the framework disappear or become less important, instead the relations between the parts of the framework are made more visible.

For instance, ERP systems make the relationship between the context and the system very concrete and complex (as shown in Fig. 10.2). The idea that the context is the starting point for ISD is, for instance, challenged. ERP systems also challenge the role of formalised methods. Almost all traditional ISD methods are built on the very basic assumption that the starting point is the present context and that the purpose of ISD is to create a system that supports the context. ERP development needs other approaches and formalised methods that recognise and accept the changed preconditions.

On the other hand, the method-in-action is still at the very core of ERP development. The need for a methodological and structured way to deal with the inherent complexity of ERP systems in practice, makes method-in-action a core notion in ERP development.

10.4   THE FRAMEWORK-IN-ACTION: WEB DEVELOPMENT

Initially, the Internet and the World Wide Web were seen as a means of communicating and sharing information across a widely dispersed audience. Creating formats to organise and display this information was the initial challenge to ISD. As the use of the web moved from the static display of information (such as an on-line brochure), to dynamic information provision and to real-time interactive applications, the challenges increased.

When creating applications for the web, developers are limited to a given—but rapidly changing—technology. It is limited because it is built as an infrastructure with the purpose of being a global standardised technology which allows for open access. The architecture and functionality of the technology are to a great extent known by every developer, although developments of the infrastructure are continuous. The standardised character of the technology limits the developer's possibilities, but also frees the developer from the responsibility for determining the appropriate technological platform.

However, although the technology for web development is quite fixed, the *user population* for these applications is much more difficult to define compared to traditional information system development. For Internet-based systems, the users of the web system could be anyone anywhere, since the system is open to the world. So, previous conceptions of how to elicit user requirements no longer apply. (Of course, in the case of internal closed corporate web-based systems, often called intranets, the user base is much more clearly defined.)

Web systems development is summarised in Fig. 10.3. The relevant components of the framework are discussed below.

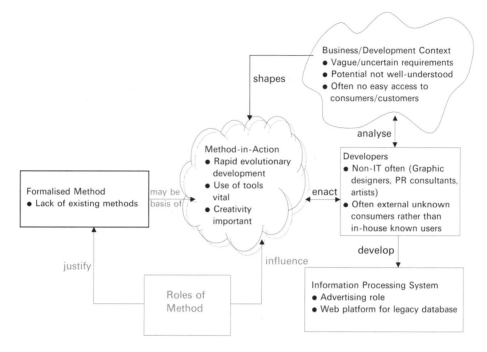

Fig. 10.3   Web Systems Development

10.4.1 Web Development Context

When the web was first introduced, it was not immediately obvious what purposes it could serve. Not only did organisations not know how to use it, but they did not know what was possible. Therefore, no one could really say what was needed or what to aim for. Requirements analysis suddenly meant something very different and raised new questions. When the developer tried to formulate organisational needs for a web system they ended up with vague requirements, often with a lot of references to the importance of keeping up with the fast pace of technological development. Organisations started out by assuming the web was the technology to use when it came to disseminating information to customers and consumers. In many cases the basic idea was that the web constituted a new and efficient form for advertising new products and for reaching new customers. The goal was simply to have a 'web presence', rather than to replace any traditional information system or to provide new functionality.

This focus on information and advertising did set the stage for the early web development contexts. A different development practice evolved where new competencies and skills were needed. Web development became more influenced by other areas such as advertising and graphic design. As compared to traditional information systems, web sites were expected to be entertaining, and their role as a mechanism for promoting and drawing people to the site became a consideration in the development process. This new context of web development presented a strong challenge to traditional ISD.

Today, the web has become more 'business as usual' for many organisations. The organisational context is more professional, more people understand the capabilities of web systems. Web systems are increasingly part of the basic systems portfolio of any organisation. They are moving even further into the core of organisations since web systems are seen as the fundamental structure for almost all information systems.

But even if web development is more traditional nowadays, there are still some aspects that are significantly different from traditional ISD. One of the most important aspects is that web development is usually aimed at systems for an unknown and extremely diverse set of users. Many web systems are not designed for professionals who will use them as a tool in their everyday work (although of course they can be), but for people who use the system to achieve something for themselves. Their use is probably sporadic and not followed by any kind of introduction or training. These new conditions still constitute a challenge to traditional ISD and will lead to new developments in ISD methods and approaches.

10.4.2 Web Developers

Since there were no traditional comparable contexts to define what kind of skills were needed, early web development attracted a diverse set of developers. Individuals with a graphics background got involved because of the focus on the visual, public relations people became interested because of the marketing aspects, etc. Early studies of web development found that the majority of web development was done by non-specialists, in fact, primarily by individuals without any IT background or formal training (Russo & Misic, 1998). As web development projects got bigger, more expertise and more people were required, and the specific focused skills were supplemented with a focus on teamwork.

Now, as web development is creating core business systems, the role of the web developer has become more professional, more structured, more organised, more complex, and more common. Whereas originally web developers were primarily self-taught, now we see formal education programs for web developers. We also see specialisation among web developer roles.

As web development becomes more structured and more complex the need for structure and organisation in the development process also grows. There is also an increased awareness of technical issues, such as security, reliability, and robustness that has had impact on the competence of web developers. Web developers today face more or less the same tasks as the traditional IS developer, but within a different context and resulting in a different type of product.

10.4.3 Web Systems

Web systems are developed for a given infrastructure and a standardised architecture. Such a stable foundation restricts the technological possibilities. A standardised infrastructure is a pre-condition for global systems with the purpose of reaching all varieties of computers and peripherals. So, even if the web is understood as a new technology it is also a technology based on a global standardisation that restricts developers in their choice of technological solutions. However, although the technology is fixed, new capabilities are introduced frequently.

Even though the technology remains the same, there has been a drastic change in the kinds of web systems developed. The first attempts were systems characterised by a static display of information. Later there was a transition to dynamic information provision, and currently, real-time interactive applications are typical. At the same time as the web systems have become more sophisticated in the area of human-computer interaction, they have also evolved 'behind the scenes' to become large database transaction handling systems.

One of the major challenges today is to find ways to create seamless systems that combine the older, internal, task-focused, systems with new web systems focused on customers and communication. This challenge is further enhanced by the presence of ERP systems and Open Source Software. Web systems have already come a long way from the first attempts at displaying information to the situation where the web constitutes the single overarching technological platform that is supposed to bring together all other technologies into one composition. The simplicity that made the web a tool at almost anyone's disposal is displaced by the need for it to be a tool for handling extraordinary complexity.

10.4.4 Web Development Method-in-Action

Web development has led to changes for the developer, the context, and the system, and has influenced the nature of the method-in-action in most organisations.

Web development presents us with a new context. When it comes to web systems there is often a radical difference between the context of development and the context of use. Web systems are not necessarily developed for a specific group of users in a known work context. Users can instead be using their home computer to buy products or services or to find information for their personal or private life. Traditional ISD is not designed to address that kind of context.

There are also other factors pushing for new practices. Since the systems have other purposes, for instance, in terms of the speed-to-market required in this environment, the context of development changes. Parallel development is necessary to meet this challenge, but existing methods do not account for this. The release orientation requires a method that supports this iterative approach (as we saw in the Rational

Unified Process in Chapter 4) as well as version control and change management (as we saw in open source software). The speed and the nature of the technology force a dependence on tools (Baskerville & Pries-Heje, 2001).

Another aspect of the context is the customer (as opposed to the more traditional 'user') involvement. Customers typically have a high level of involvement in the content and look-and-feel of the web sites being developed for them. Frequent prototyping can be part of this interactive development with the customer. There is typically no interaction, however, with users in the first iteration of the web system. (There may be some limited feedback after the system goes into operation.) Thus, in the initial design, only vague requirements exist, either due to the lack of contact with potential users, or due to customer uncertainty as to what they want or need, or both.

In terms of the system itself, the architecture is critical and, in most cases, fixed (until a change in platform occurs). Developers no longer have a choice regarding the particular platform, but focus more on the creative aspects. The requirement to very rapidly produce new releases as well as the technology itself lend themselves to a component-based structuring of web systems.

Although there are many differences between web system development and traditional information systems development, this is not to say that there is a totally different process at work. Whereas the ability to instantly publish a web application appears to "trivialise" the need for planning and design (Balasubramanian & Bashian, 1998), experience has shown that insofar as web applications are computer-based information systems, general systems development principles apply (Dennis, 1998). Although the means for completing the tasks might differ, both web system development and traditional information system development require many of the same types of activities. In both environments, there is a need to define information and processing requirements, to design the interface, and to build, test, and maintain the system. The importance of good database design, for example, cannot be ignored.

However, the old traditional modes of development alone are no longer sufficient in the web environment. Support for creativity and innovation and a broader understanding of the user population are required. The method-in-action must be flexible to support this emergent area.

10.5   CHAPTER SUMMARY

This chapter has drawn upon our framework to model a number of development scenarios relevant to today's development environment. These were open source software, ERP systems development, and web development.

In the case of open source software, we illustrated the common trend whereby OSS products tend to be produced initially to satisfy some personal problem of an individual developer, and then grow as other developers also find the product potentially useful. However, the system requirements are more or less universally shared and taken for granted, a necessary precondition if large numbers of developers are to collaborate on development without ever necessarily meeting face-to-face. Also, OSS developers tend to be creative and passionate hackers who are motivated by a strong ideological belief in what they are doing, and are reinforced by the sense of belonging to a community of respected peers. The majority are professional developers rather than amateur hobbyists operating from their bedrooms. Most OSS products also fall into the category of technical infra-structural support systems, which are selected by a very technically-literate consumer base. Also, while many have suggested the 'bazaar' of the OSS development model is not compatible with the 'cathedral' of a formalised method, it is apparent that some fundamental principles of ISD—modularity, information-hiding, configuration management and independent peer review—are very much a feature of OSS development. Indeed, peer review in OSS is taken to a new level in terms of its globality and truly independent nature. However, the method-in-action is very much premised around the bazaar of independent personal development approaches. Much duplication of effort may take place, with different developers working on the same aspects of the system. However, the evolutionary principle of 'survival of the fittest' ensures that a greater range of possible options are considered and the most viable one chosen.

The chapter also considered ERP systems, and the impact of this class of software on system development in organisations. The implementation of ERP systems, to a greater degree even than other package software, typically requires a great deal of customisation to configure the software to meet the needs of the particular organisational context. Some organisations actually find it more feasible to change their own business processes to match the default processes built into the ERP software. Thus, rather than developing a system to meet the requirements of the organisation, the organisational processes are changed to meet the requirements of the purchased software. Obviously the need for method support is quite different in this type of environment. Very little new development is done, and what little is done is restricted to developing interfaces between the ERP system and remaining legacy systems.

Finally, the chapter investigated the nature of web development. Web development is not old, but its short history has shown how a new technology, which at first radically challenged the traditional ISD, is now being incorporated into a bigger picture. Web development has changed from being a 'hip' technology to becoming a very fundamental technology bringing all other technologies together. Recent history also shows how ideas about competence quickly changes. Web development today demands all traditional ISD skills, plus some new skills that have to be included in the repertoire.

The three scenarios all challenge some or many aspects of ISD. At the same time we do believe that they all correspond to some degree to the core content and structure of the framework. New scenarios do present new ideas, new procedures, new technologies, but at the core there is still a development process and a developer facing more or less the same difficulties and challenges.

An overall conclusion from the chapter is that the framework makes it possible to analyse and understand the distinct features and unique aspects of new approaches to ISD. It also shows the rich variety and deep differences among the various approaches to ISD. The diversity in ISD today creates a challenge to the practicing developer and to the organisation having to choose an approach. The need for a broad and inclusive framework for understanding modern ISD is obvious, and we believe this book provides such a framework.

10.6   DISCUSSION QUESTIONS

1.   ERP systems are designed to cover almost all information systems needs in an organisation. How does this affect ISD, and how does it influence the competence of the developer?

2.   In the early days of the web, the development process attracted people with a diverse set of skills, not always based on formal education in IS. Is this typical when new technologies enter the market? How can a professional IS developer prepare for new technological challenges?

3.   OSS is a very different way of producing software. What do you see as the driving force behind this development? And is it a challenge to the software industry?

4.   In this chapter we have discussed some scenarios that in different ways challenge traditional ISD. Are there other challenges? And what might be more radical challenges in the future?

5.   It seems that the scenarios presented in this chapter are very different. Is there, and will there be, anything that holds ISD together as a professional practice? What do you see as the skills overlapping all presented scenarios?

11

Conclusion

This book is premised on the belief that IS development is at the core of the IS field. New information systems are developed all the time. New technology, new knowledge, a changing world—all these force organisations to change, or at least to make intentional decisions as to how to relate to and deal with the changing environment. To most organisations this means that they must themselves change, and this is often accomplished by using new technological systems.

In this book we argue that the creation of these new systems is the core activity, and that this has not changed even though the preconditions for ISD has radically been transformed. ISD may not be a specific activity which can be easily isolated within an organisation. It does not always take the form of the traditional in-house systems development project. Instead, it can manifest itself in many diverse ways.

To be a professional IS developer today means that one has to understand the complexity and novelty of this situation. It means that one has to understand in what forms ISD can be found, and what kinds of activities are involved. Such an understanding is needed in order to determine what is expected from one as a professional and what competence is needed. This book is about creating such a broad understanding, and providing a stable conceptual 'map' of the practice of ISD. We achieve this by focusing on methods and on how they can be used and understood, both in research and practice, i.e. the focus is method-in-action. It is necessary to find a foundation, a conceptual 'map', that will allow for new ways of understanding ISD to evolve.

One of the problems in the field today is that ISD research, though valuable in many ways, is not brought together in a synthesis that might act as a support for other researchers and practitioners. One conclusion is therefore that there is a need for a broad conceptual framework for ISD, but one which is also readily accessible and usable by all stakeholders, both academic and practitioner. Our purpose with this book is to provide such a framework. We harbour no illusions that our proposal is entirely comprehensive or completely correct, but we believe it can at least serve as a foundation for a dialogue to produce a 'better' model.

Any understanding of ISD as a field of knowledge must be built on an understanding of the history of the practice of the field. We have provided a historical perspective of ISD practice in this book, by means of a detailed account of the dominant issues and methods within ISD for the past four decades of its existence. We ourselves have discovered that a historical perspective reveals not just how much has happened, but also how little has changed. Many of the fundamental ideas in ISD are 'old'. Now and then some of these ideas are re-formulated and 'sold' again as new solutions to new problems. The historical perspective gives us valuable knowledge on the development of ideas, and what is real change. Also, it helps us to evaluate new approaches, methods, and technologies. This is why we have given the history of ISD so much space in this book, even though our goal is also to be up-to-date, presenting the most recent developments in the field. Over time, there have been many attempts (ERP, BPR, OSS, and countless other acronyms) to reformulate the core by means of some new framework, but none have so far succeeded. We believe the core remains the same. It contains the same kind of timeless problems. To learn about these problems requires a detailed knowledge of how these problems were addressed in the past in our field.

Education within ISD should be based on a stable framework that reveals the large canvas necessary to take account of all the important issues in ISD. We believe our framework can be used as a tool in teaching the practice of ISD, and that it will help students and practitioners to position methods and techniques, formal and informal traditions and guidelines, new and old development approaches, in relation to each other. Each individual section of the book, whether it is concerned with a specific method or approach, is not nearly enough from a practical perspective. Nevertheless, it should serve as an anchoring mechanism on which to 'hang' the necessary knowledge.

The framework can also work as a foundation for synthesising previous and current research. Most topics related to ISD can be located within the framework, thus it can help build on earlier knowledge in the field. We also hope it can stimulate new research in ISD. With the framework in place, new ideas and theories concerning the development and importance of methods can be analysed and developed. Methods may be viewed not only as instruments guiding action, but also as holders of experience and knowledge, carriers of theories and concepts for the field, instruments for learning, etc.

The framework can also work as a tool for reflection for practitioners in the field. We consider ourselves to be 'practicing reflectors,' but adopting this terminology also implies that we subscribe to the 'reflective practitioner' concept. Our strong support for the role and contribution of human stakeholders in the ISD process reveals our faith in human capability. We have sufficient experience of real development practice to know that practitioners have usually been able to solve development problems without waiting for the often unwieldy advice of academic researchers. The area of ISD is one in which many advances have first appeared in development practice—compiler design, user interface design, programming style, prototyping, business process reengineering, open source software, to name but a few. These advances have obviously been the work of 'reflective practitioners,' and they have been subsequently reified into 'valid' research issues which have then attracted an abundance of academic research. Often they have been treated as somewhat heretic at first, but the stubborn persistence of practitioners to use what works has ensured that they survived.

Prototyping is an obvious case in point. In the early 1980s, the conventional wisdom suggested that developers should always specify system requirements completely in advance, the rationale being that changes of mind were very costly to rectify later in the development process. On a personal note, one of us can recall developing systems in the early 1980s and struggling to finalise requirements which could then be signed off by users prior to commencing actual design and programming. Time and again, he failed in this regard. He attributed this to personal deficiencies (and undoubtedly this may have been right to a large extent!), but would comfort himself by vowing to finalise and sign-off requirements next time. Of course, he never achieved this. However, about 1985, he stumbled across an article in a computing journal about something called 'prototyping'. It described precisely what he had been doing for years, and suggested that it had particular strengths, and was, indeed, the way of the future. Galvanised by this, he happily prototyped his way through all subsequent development projects, until he finally made his most significant contribution to systems development (until this book obviously), when he abandoned its commercial practice.

Anyway, the point of the above is that many developers, being good reflective practitioners, had worked out the benefits of prototyping and were happy to indulge in this 'heresy.' In time, the principle of prototyping became 'sanctified' in the various ISD methods being promoted.

The work presented in this book is to a large extent built on empirical and theoretical research done by us and many other researchers. It is not based on one simplistic idea fashioned into some kind of all-encompassing principle, as is the case perhaps with some of the management literature. It is not based on esoteric theoretical abstractions, nor is it based solely on common sense and everyday experience. We do believe it is founded on a reasonably sound understanding of the practice of ISD as seen through the best research knowledge so far developed in the field. This means that it is a book that presents some basic conclusions on the nature of ISD. Below we briefly summarise some of these conclusions.

First of all, ISD is always situated. Every development project is unique. This means that a detailed prescriptive approach will never completely address all the problems encountered by a practitioner. The practitioner will always be the one making the decisions and judgements which determine whether the project is successful or not. Whether or not a specific project is successful is also something that can only be determined in relation to the specifics of the situation. Theoretical or methodological support for the developer can only inform decisions and judgements, and provide guidance by indicating possible dangers and opportunities.

Another basic conclusion—one that this book rests upon—is that ISD research should be focused on method-in-action. ISD is a practice, and as such it is something characterised by extreme complexity and richness. It is not an activity which can be fully described or understood. ISD is not about methods which are built on ideals from a one-dimensional understanding of reality. ISD has to cope with the richness present in every unique project. Method-in-action is the concept we use to make this basic and real aspect of practice visible and in focus.

Method-in-action is the object of study and the practice is ISD. This means that new ideas and new knowledge have to be built in close relation to existing practice. History shows us over and over again that new ideas, if not grounded in practice, have seldom made any real change in that practice. Good ideas and new theories have to be based on a deep understanding of the preconditions of ISD in real organisations. History also reveals a number of 'good' ideas, methods, and techniques that worked well in laboratories or in research settings but never were implemented successfully in real practice.

The IS field is constantly faced with new technology, new ideas, new methods, new organisational and management approaches, all claiming to be the ultimate solution—usually accompanied by the claim that ISD will not be necessary anymore. This is not our belief. Instead, we hope that even if this book does not answer all questions it will at least bring ISD back to where it belongs. It will hopefully influence researchers, practitioners and students to devote more time to the study of the practice of ISD. The final message from this book is that information systems development is still at the core the field, and will be so for a long time.

References

Alavi, M. (1984) An assessment of the prototyping approach to information systems development. *Communications of the ACM*, **June**, 556–563.

Alexander, C. (1964) *Notes on the Synthesis of Form*, Harvard University Press, Cambridge.

Andersen, P. and Mathiassen, L. (1987) Systems development and use: a science of truth or a theory of lies, in Bjerknes, G., Ehn, P., and King, M. (eds) *Computers and Democracy: A Scandinavian Challenge*. Avebury Gower, Brookfield Vermont.

Argyris, C. and Schon, D. (1974) *Theory in Practice: Increasing Professional Effectiveness*, Jossey-Bass, USA.

Avison, D., Fitzgerald, G. and Wood-Harper, A. (1988) Information systems development: a tool kit is not enough. *The Computer Journal*, **31**, 4, 379–380.

Avison, D., Golder, P. and Shah, H. (1992) A toolkit for soft systems methodology, in Kendall, K, Lyytinen, K. and DeGross, H. (eds) (1992) *The Impact of Computer Supported Technologies on IS Development*, Elsevier Publishers, North Holland, 273–287.

Avison, D. and Wood-Harper, A. (1990) *Multiview: An Exploration in Information Systems Development*, Blackwell Scientific Publications, Oxford.

Avison, D.E. & Fitzgerald, G. (1995) *Information Systems Development: Methodologies, Techniques and Tools*. McGraw-Hill Companies, London.

Avison, D.E., Wood-Harper, A.T., Vidgen, R.T., and Wood, J.R.G. (1998) A further exploration into information systems development: the evolution of Multiview 2. *Information Technology & People*, **11**, 2, 124–139.

Bach, J. (1994) The immaturity of the CMM, *American Programmer*, Vol. 7, No. 9, pp. 13–18.

Baker, F. (1972) "Chief Programmer Team management of Production Programming", *IBM Systems Journal*, 11:1, pp. 56–73.

Balasubramanian, V. and Bashian, A. (1998) Document management and web technologies: Alice marries the Mad Hatter, *Communications of the ACM*, **41**, 7, 107–115.

Bansler, J. and Bodker, K. (1993) A reappraisal of structured analysis: design in an organisational context, *ACM Transactions on Information Systems*, **11**, 2, 165–193.

Barnhart, A. (2001) Process for sale, *Software Development*, **June**, 35–37.

Baskerville, R. and Pries-Heje, J. (2001) Racing the e-bomb: how the Internet is redefining information systems development methodology, in Russo, N.L., Fitzgerald, B. and DeGross, J.I. (eds), *Realigning Research and Practice in Information Systems Development: The Social and Organizational Perspective*, Kluwer Academic Publishers, Boston, MA, 49–68.

Bateson, G. (1972) *Steps to an Ecology of Mind*, Ballantine Books, New York.

Baum, D. (1992) Go totally RAD and build applications faster, *Datamation*, September, pp. 79–81.

Beck, K. (2000) *Extreme Programming Explained*. Addison Wesley, MA.

Benyon, D. and Skidmore, S. (1987) Towards a toolkit for the systems analyst. *The Computer Journal*, **30**, 1, 2–7.

Berard, E. (1995) Object-oriented methodologies, Online document available at http://www.toa.com.

Bergland, G. (1981) A guided tour of program design methodologies, *IEEE Computer*, **October**, 13–37.

Berrisford & Wetherbe, (1979).

Beynon-Davies, P. (1989) *Information Systems Development*, Macmillan, London.

Beynon-Davies, P. Tudhope, D. and Mackay, H. (1997), Integrating RAD and participatory design, in Avison, D. (ed.) *Key Issues in Information Systems*, McGraw-Hill, UK, pp. 317–330.

Beynon-Davies, P. Carne, C. Mackay, H. and Tudhope, D. (1998), A comparison of seven RAD projects, in Avison, D. and Edgar-Nevill, D. (eds) Matching Technology with Organisational Needs, McGraw-Hill, UK, pp. 127–140.

Beynon-Davies, P. (1989) *Information Systems Development, Macmillan*, London.

Bezroukov, N. (1999) "Open Source Software as a Special Type of Academic Research (A Critique of Vulgar Raymondism)", *First Monday*, 4:10.

Bjorn-Andersen, N. (1988) Are 'human factors' human?, *The Computer Journal*, **31**, 5, 386–390.

Boehm, B. (1976) Software engineering. *IEEE Transactions on Computers*, **25**, 12, 1226–1241.

Boehm, B. (1981) Software Engineering Economics. Prentice Hall, Englewood Cliffs, New Jersey.

Boehm, B. (1988) A spiral model of software development and maintenance. *IEEE Computer*, **21**, 5, 61–72.

Bohm, C. and Jacopini, G. (1966). Flow diagrams, Turing machines and languages with only two formation rules. *Communications of the ACM*, **May**, 366–371.

Bollinger, T. and McGowan, C. (1991) A critical look at software capability evaluations. *IEEE Software*, **July**, 25–41.

Booch, G., Rumbaugh, J., and Jacobson, I. (1998) *Unified Modeling Language User Guide*, Addison-Wesley, Reading, MA.

Booch, G., Jacobson, I. and Rumbaugh, J. (1998). *Unified Modeling Language 1.3*, White paper, Rational Software Corp., 1998.

Brooks, F. (1987) No silver bullet: essence and accidents of software engineering. *IEEE Computer Magazine*, **April**, 10–19.

Brooks, F. (1975) *The Mythical Man-Month*, USA: Addison-Wesley.

Bubenko, J. (1986) Information system methodologies – a research view. In Olle *et al.*, (1986) *Information Systems Design Methodologies: Improving the Practice*, North-Holland, 289–318.

Buckingham, R., Hirschheim, R., Land, F. and Tully, C. (eds) (1987) *Information Systems Education: Recommendations and Implementation*, Cambridge University Press, Cambridge.

Business Week (1988) The software trap: automate—or else, *Business Week*, May 9, 142–154.

Butler, T. (2000) Transforming information systems development through computer-aided systems engineering (CASE): lessons from practice, *Information Systems Journal*, Vol. 10, No. 3, pp. 167–193.

Butler, T. and Fitzgerald, B. (1998) The institutionalisation of user participation for systems development in Telecom Eireann, *Annals of Cases on Information Technology*, 1, 68–86.

Cameron, J. (1986) An overview of JSD, IEEE *Transactions on Software Engineering*, **SE-12**, 2, 222–240.

Canning, R. (1956). in Agresti, W. (1986) *New Paradigms for Software Development*. IEEE Computer Society Press, Washington DC.

Card, D. (1995) The RAD fad: is timing really everything?, *IEEE Software*, September.

Chapin, N. (1980) *Flowcharts*, Auerbach, New Jersey.

Checkland, P. (1999) *Soft Systems Methodology in Action*, Wiley, Chichester.

Checkland, P. (1981) *Systems Thinking, Systems Practice*, Wiley, Chichester.

Checkland, P., & Scholes, J. (1990) *Soft Systems in Action*. Wiley, Chichester.

Chen, P. (1976) The entity relationship model—towards a unified view of data, *ACM Transactions on Database Systems*, **1**, 1, 9–36.

Chikofsky, E. (1989) How to lose productivity with productivity tools. *Proceedings of 3rd IFAC/IFIP Workshop*, Indiana, US, 1–4.

Ciborra, C. (2000) *From Control to Drift – The Dynamics of Corporate Information Infrastructures*. Oxford University Press, London.

Coad, P. and Yourdon, E. (1991) *Object-Oriented Analysis*, (2nd Edition), Yourdon Press, New Jersey.

Coad, P. (1993) Object-oriented analysis course notes. London 15–17 March 1993.

Colter, M. (1982) Evolution of the structured methodologies. In Couger *et al.*, (1982) *Advanced System Development Feasibility Techniques*, Wiley & Sons, New York, 73–96.

Colter, M. (1984) A comparative examination of systems analysis techniques. *MIS Quarterly*, **8**, 1, 51–66.

Constantine, L. (1989) The structured design approach. *Byte*, **April**, 232–233.

Couger, J., Colter, M. & Knapp, R. (1982) *Advanced System Development Feasibility Techniques*, Wiley & Sons, New York.

Couger, J. (1973) Evolution of business systems analysis techniques. *Computing Surveys*, **5**, 3, 167–198.

Creasy, P. and Hesse, W. (1994) Two-level NIAM – a way to get it object-oriented. In Verrijn-Stuart and Olle (eds) *Methods and Associated Tools for the IS life cycle*, IFIP North Holland, 209–222.

Crosby, P.B. (1979) *Quality is Free*, McGraw-Hill, New York.

Dahlbom, B. and Matthiassen, L. (1993) *Computers in Context: The Philosophy and Practice of Systems Design*, Blackwell, Oxford.

Davis, G. (1982) Strategies for information requirements determination. *IBM Systems Journal*, **21**, 1, 4–30.

Davis, G. and Olson, M. (1985) *Management Information Systems: Conceptual Foundations, Structure and Development*, 2nd Edition, McGraw-Hill, New York.

Davis, A., Bersoff, E. and Comer, E. (1988) A strategy for comparing alternative software development life cycle models. *IEEE Transactions on Software Engineering*, **October**, 1453–1460.

DeGrace, P and Stahl, L. (1990) *Wicked Problems, Righteous Solutions: A Catalogue of Modern Software Engineering Paradigms*. Yourdon Press, Prentice Hall, Englewood Cliffs, New Jersey.

Dearnley, P. and Mayhew, P. (1983) In favour of systems prototypes and their integration into the systems development cycle, *The Computer Journal*, **26**, 1, 36–42.

DeMarco, T. (1978) *Structured Analysis and System Specification*, Yourdon Press, New Jersey.

DeMarco, T. and Lister T. (1989) Software development: state of the art v. state of the practice. *11th International Conference on Software Engineering*, 271–275.

Deming, W.E. (1986) Out of the Crisis, Massachusettes Institute of Technology Centre for Advanced Engineering Study, Cambridge, MA.

Dennis, A. (1998) Lessons from three years of web development. *Communications of the ACM*, **41**, 7, 112–113.

Dijkstra, E. (1972) The humble programmer. In Yourdon, E. (1979) *Classics in Software Engineering*. Yourdon Press, New York.

Dijkstra, E. (1965) Programming considered as a human activity, In Yourdon, E. (1979) *Classics in Software Engineering*. Yourdon Press, New York, 3–14.

Dock, P. (1992) Object methods, *Hotline on Object-Oriented Technology*, **3**, 12, 4–6.

Downs, E., Clare, P. and Coe, I. (1992) *Structured Systems Analysis and Design Method: Application and Context*. Prentice-Hall International (UK), Hertfordshire.

DSDM (1995) *Dynamic Systems Development Method*, Tesseract Publishing, UK.

Due, R. (1992) A new object-oriented modelling paradigm. *American Programmer*, **5**, 8, 13–16.

Dyke, R. and Kunz, J. (1989) Object-oriented programming. *IBM Systems Journal*, **28**, 3.

Feller, J. and Fitzgerald, B. (2002) *Understanding Open Source Sofware Development*, Addison-Wesley, UK.

Finkelstein, C. (1989) *An Introduction to Information Engineering*, Addison-Wesley, Sydney.

Firesmith, D. (1992) Take a flying leap: the plunge into object-oriented technology. *American Programmer*, **5**, 8, 17–27.

Fitzgerald, B. (1994) The systems development dilemma: whether to adopt formalised systems development methodologies or not?, in Baets, W. (ed.) *Proceedings of the Second European Conference on Information Systems*, Nijenrode University Press, Holland, 691–706.

Fitzgerald, B. (1997) The Use of Systems Development Methodologies in Practice: A Field Study, *The Information Systems Journal*, Vol. 7, No. 3, pp. 201–212.

Fitzgerald, B. (1998) An Empirical Investigation into the Adoption of Systems Development Methodologies, *Information & Management*, Vol. 34, pp. 317–328.

Fitzgerald, B. and O'Kane, T. (1999) A Longitudinal Study of Software Process Improvement, *IEEE Software*, May/June, pp. 37–45.

Fitzgerald, B., Russo, N. and O'Kane, T. (2002) Method Tailoring at Motorola, forthcoming in *Communications of the ACM*.

Flaatten, P., McCubbrey, D., O'Riordan, P. and Burgess, K. (1989) *Foundations of Business Systems*, Dryden Press, Chicago.

Flavin, M. (1981) *Fundamental Concepts of Information Modelling*, Yourdon Press, New York.

Floyd, C. (1987) Outline of a paradigm change in software engineering. In *Computers and Democracy: A Scandinavian Challenge*. Bjerknes, G., Ehn, P., and King, M. (eds), Avebury Gower, Brookfield Vermont.

Floyd, C., Melh, W., Resin, F., Schmidt, G. and Wolf, G. (1989) Out of Scandinavia: alternative approaches to software design and system development, *Human Computer Interaction*, **4**, 253–350.

Fowler, M. (1999) *Refactoring: Improving the Design of Existing Code*, Addison-Wesley, MA.

Friedman, A. (1989) *Computer Systems Development: History, Organisation and Implementation*, Wiley & Sons, Chichester.

Gane, C. and Sarson, T. (1977) *Structured Systems Analysis: Tools and Techniques*, Improved System Technologies, New York.

Gane, C. (1989) *Rapid Systems Development*, Prentice-Hall, USA Gane, C. (1991) The triumph of the structured movement. *American Programmer*, **4**, 11, 38–39.

Gladden, G. (1982) Stop the life-cycle, I want to get off, *ACM SIGSOFT Software Engineering Notes*, **7**, 2.

Glass, R. (1977) *The Universal Elixir and Other Computing Projects Which Failed*, Computing Trends, Seattle.

Glass, R. (1991) *Software Conflict: Essays on the Art and Science of Software Engineering*. Yourdon Press, Prentice Hall, Englewood Cliffs, New Jersey.

Glass, R.L. (1998) "Is there really a software crisis?" *IEEE Software*, Vol. 15, No. 1, pp. 104–105.

Gremillion, L. and Pyburn, P. (1983) Breaking the systems development bottleneck. *Harvard Business Review*, **March/April**, 130–137.

Hackathorn, R. and Karimi, J. (1988) A framework for comparing information engineering methods. *MIS Quarterly*, **June**, 202–220.

Harel, E. and McLean, E. (1985) The effects of using a non-procedural language on programmer productivity, *MIS Quarterly*, **9**, 2, 109–120.

Hargrave, D. (1995) *SSADM 4+ for Rapid Systems Development*, McGraw-Hill, UK.

Harmesen, F., Brinkkemper, S. and Oei, H. (1994) Situational method engineering for IS project approaches, in Verrijn-Stuart, A. & Olle, T. (eds) *Methods and Associated Tools for the IS Life Cycle*, Elsevier Science, North-Holland, 169–194.

Hatley, D. and Pirbhai, I. (1988) *Strategies for Real-Time System Specification*, Dorset House, New York.

Henson, K. and Hughes, C. (1991) A two-dimensional approach to systems development. *Journal of Information Systems Management*, **Winter**, 35–43.

Highsmith, J. (2000) *Adaptive Software Development*, Dorset House, New York.

Highsmith, J. and Cockburn, A. (2001) Agile software development: the business of innovation, *Computer*, September, pp. 120–122.

Hirschheim, R. and Klein, H. (1989) Four paradigms of information systems development, *Communications of the ACM*, **32**, 10, 1199–1216.

Hirschheim, R. (1985a) User experience with and assessment of participative systems design. *MIS Quarterly*, **December**, 295–304.

Hirschheim, R. (1983) Assessing participative systems design: some conclusions from an exploratory study, *Information & Management*, **6**, 6, 317–327.

Holloway, S. (1989) *Methodology Handbook for Information Managers*, Gower Technical, Aldershot.

Hough, D. (1993) Rapid delivery: an evolutionary approach for application development, *IBM Systems Journal*, **32**, 3, 397–419.

Howard, R. (1985) UTOPIA: where workers craft new technology. *Technology Review*, **28**, 3.

Howe, D. (1984) *Data Analysis for Data Base Design*, Edward Arnold, London.

Humphrey, W.S. and Sweet, W.L. (1987) A Method for Assessing the Software Engineering Capability of Contractors, SEI-87-TR-23, *Software Engineering Institute*, Carnegie Mellon University, Pittsburgh, Pennsylvania.

Humphrey, W.S., (1988) Characterizing the Software Process: A Maturity Framework, *IEEE Software*, **March**.

IEEE (1991) *Standard for Developing Software Life Cycle Processes*, IEEE Computer Society, 345 East 47th St., New York., P1074/D6.1.

Iivari, J. and Koskela, E. (1987) The PIOCO model for information systems design, *MIS Quarterly*, **September**, 400–419.

Iivari, J. (1989) A methodology for IS development as organisational change. In Klein, H. and Kumar, K. (1989) *Systems Development for Human Progress*, North-Holland, Amsterdam, 197–217.

Ingevaldsson, L. (1979) *JSP: A Practical Method of Program Design*, Studentlitteratur, Lund.

Jackson, M. (1975) *Principles of Program Design*, Academic Press, London.

Jackson, M. (1983) *System Development*, Prentice-Hall, New Jersey.

Jayaratna, N. (1994) *Understanding and Evaluating Methodologies*, McGraw-Hill, London.

Jenkins, A., Naumann, J. and Wetherbe, J. (1984) Empirical investigation of systems development practices and results. *Information & Management*, **7**, 73–82.

Jones, M. and Walsham, G. (1992) The limits of the knowable: organizational and design knowledge in system development. In Kendall, K., DeGross, J. and Lyytinen, K. (eds) *The Impact of Computer Supported Technologies on Information Systems Development*, Elsevier Science Publishers B.V., North Holland Press, 195–213.

Juran, J.M. (1988) *Planning for Quality*, Macmillan, NewYork.

Juran, J.M. (1989) *Leadership for Quality*, The Free Press, New York.

Kautz, K. (1998) Software process improvement in very small enterprises: does it pay off? *Software Process: Improvement and Practice*, Vol. 4, pp. 209–226.

Keen, P. and Scott Morton, M. (1978) *Decision Support Systems: An Organizational Perspective*, Addison-Wesley, Reading.

King, M. and Pardoe, J. (1985) *Program Design using JSP: A Practical Introduction*, Macmillan, London.

King, D. (1984) *Current Practices in Software Development*, Yourdon Press, New Jersey.

Kozar, K. (1989) Adopting systems development methods: an exploratory study. *Journal of Management Information Systems*, **5**, 4, 73–86.

Krutchen, P. (1996) A rational development process, *Crosstalk*, 9, 7, 11–16.

Kruchten, P. (2000) *Rational Unified Process-An Introduction*, Addison-Wesley, Reading, MA.

Kumar, K. and Welke, R. (1992) Methodology engineering: a proposal for situation-specific methodology construction, in Cotterman, W. and Senn, J. (eds) *Challenges and Strategies for Research in Systems Development*, Wiley & Sons, Chichester.

Kuwabara, K. (2000) "Linux: A Bazaar at the Edge of Chaos", *First Monday*, 5:3, http://firstmonday.org/issues/issue5_3/kuwabara/index.html, Last Accessed June 22, 2001.

Land, F., Mumford, E. and Hawgood, J. (1980) Training the systems analyst of the 1980s: four analytical procedures to assist the design process. In Lucas, H., Land, F., Lincoln, and Supper (eds) *The Information Systems Environment*, North Holland Press, 239–256.

Langefors, B. (1973) *Theoretical Analysis of Information Systems*, Auerbach, Philadelphia.

Lecht, C. (1977) *The Waves of Change*, McGraw-Hill, New York.

Lee, J. and Kim, S. (1992) The relationship btween procedural formalisation and MIS success. *Information & Management*, **22**, 89–111.

Lee, B. (1979) *Introducing Systems Analysis and Design*, NCC Publications, UK.

Lehtinen, E. and Lyytinen, K. (1984) Discourse analysis as an information system specification method, *Proceedings of the Seventh Scandinavian Research Seminar on Systemeering*, Helsinki.

Leonard, A. (2000) *Salon Free Software Project*, http://www.salon.com/tech/fsp/, Last Accessed June 23, 2001.

Leonard-Barton, D. (1987) Implementing structured software methodologies: a case of innovation in process technology. *Interfaces*, **17**, 3, 6–17.

Lewis, T. (1999) The Open Source Acid Test. *IEEE Computer*, Feb 1999.

Longworth, G. (1985) *Designing Systems for Change*. NCC, Manchester.

Lundeberg, M. (1982) The ISAC approach to specification in information systems etc. In Olle *et al.* (eds) (1982) *Information Systems Design Methodologies: A Comparative Review*, North-Holland, 173–234.

Lyytinen, K. (1987) A taxonomic perspective on information systems development, in Boland, R and Hirschheim, R. (eds) *Critical Issues in Information Systems Research*, John Wiley and Sons, Chichester.

Markus, L., Manville, B. and Agres, C. (2000) What makes a virtual organization work? *Sloan Management Review*, Vol. 42, No. 1, 13–26.

Martin, J. and Finkelstein, C. (1981) *Information Engineering*, Savant Institute, UK.

Martin, J. (1982a) *Strategic Data-Planning Methodologies*, Prentice-Hall, Englewood Cliffs.

Martin, J. (1984) *An Information Systems Manifesto*, Prentice-Hall, Englewood Cliffs.

Martin, J. and Odell, J. (1992) *Object-Oriented Analysis & Design*, Prentice-Hall, Englewood Cliffs.

Martin, J. (1991) *Rapid Application Development*, Macmillan, USA.

Martin, J. (1989) *Information Engineering*. Prentice Hall, Englewood Cliffs, New Jersey.

Mathiassen, L., Munk-Madsen, A., Nielsen, P.A., Stage, J. (2000) *Object Oriented Analysis & Design*, Marko Publishing ApS, Aalborg, Denmark.

Maynard, H. and Stegemerten, G. (1939) *Operational Analysis*, McGraw-Hill, New York.

McConnell, S. 1999. Open Source Methodology: Ready for Prime Time? *IEEE Software*, **Jul/ Aug** 1999.

McCracken, D. and Jackson, M. (1981) A minority dissenting position. In Agresti, W. (1986) *New Paradigms for Software Development*. IEEE Computer Society Press, Washington DC.

McMenamin, S. and Palmer, J. (1984) *Essential Systems Analysis*, Yourdon Press, Prentice Hall, Englewood Cliffs, New Jersey.

Mills, H. (1971) Chief programmer teams: principles and procedures, IBM Federal Systems Division, Gaithersburg, US.

Mimno, P. (1991) What is RAD?, *American Programmer*, **4**, 1.

Monarchi, D. and Puhr, G. (1992) A research typology for OO analysis and design. *Communications of the ACM*, **35**, 9, 35–47.

Mumford, E. and Weir, M (1979) *Computer Systems in Work Design—The ETHICS Method*, Associated Business Press.

Mumford, E. (1984) Participation- from Aristotle to today. In Bemelmans, T. (ed.) *Beyond Productivity: Information Systems Development for Organisational Effectiveness*, Elsevier Science Publishers B.V., North Holland Press, 95–104.

Mumford, E., Land, F. and Hawgood, J. (1978) A participative approach to the design of computer systems, *Impact on Society*, Vol. 25, No. 3, pp. 235–253.

Mumford, E. (1983) *Designing Human Systems*, Manchester Business School, Manchester.

Naur, P. Randell, B. and Buxton, J. (1976) *Software Engineering: Concepts and Techniques*, Charter Publishers, New York.

Netcraft (2001) "The Netcraft Web Server Survey", http://www.netcraft.com/survey/, Last Accessed April 24, 2001.

O'Kane, T. (1999) The Management of a Software Process Improvement Program in a Large Softwre Organisation, Unpublished Masters thesis, University College Cork, Ireland.

O'Reilly, T. (2000) "Open Source: The Model for Collaboration in the Age of the Internet," Wide Open News, http://www.wideopen.com/reprint/740.html (May 1, 2000).

Oliga, J. (1988) Methodological foundations of systems methodologies, *Systems Practice*, **1**, 1, 87–112.

Olle, T., Verrijn-Stuart, A. and Bhabuta, L. (1988) *Computerized Assistance During the Information Life Cycle*, North Holland.

Oppelland, H. (1984) Participative information systems development: experiences with the PORGI methodology, in Bemelmans, T. (ed.) *Beyond Productivity: Information Systems Development for Organisational Effectiveness*, Elsevier Science Publishers B.V., North Holland Press, 105–121.

Orr, K. (1977) *Structured Systems Development*, Yourdon Press, New York.

Orr, K. (1989) Methodology: the experts speak. *BYTE*, **April**, 221–233.

Palmer, J. (1991) Move over structured stuff. Here comes the meta techniques. *American Programmer*, **4**, 11, 17–22.

Palmer, I. and Rock-Evans, R. (1981) *Data Analysis*, IPC Publications, Surrey.

Palvia, P. and Nosek, J. (1993) A field examination of system life cycle techniques and methodologies. *Information & Management*, **25**, 73–84.

Parnas, D. and Clements, P. (1986) A rational design process: how and why to fake it. *IEEE Transactions on Software Engineering*, **February**, 251–257.

Parnas, D. (1972) On the criteria to be used in decomposing systems into modules. *Communications of the ACM*, **15**, 12, 1053–1058.

Paulk, M.C. (1995) "The Evolution of the SEI's Capability Maturity Model for Software", *Software Improvement and Practice*, Pilot Issue, ISSN 1077-4866, SPIPFL 1(PI) 1–78 (1995), John Wiley & Sons.

Paulk, M., Curtis, B., Chrissis, M. and Weber C. (1993) Capability Maturity Model for Software, version 1.1, IEEE Software, Vol. 10, No. 4, pp. 18–27.

Peters, L. and Tripp, L. (1977) Comparing software design methodologies. *Datamation*, **November**, 89–94.

Peters, L. (1981) *Software Design: Methods and Techniques*. Yourdon Press, New York.

Plat, N., Katwijk, J. and Pronk, K. (1991) A case for structured analysis/formal design. In *VDM '91: Formal Software Development Methods*, Prehn, S. and Toetenel, W. (eds), Vol. 1, Springer-Verlag.

Poppendieck, M. (2001) Lean programming: part 2, *Software Development*, June 2001, pp. 71–75.

Pressman, R. (1987) *Software Engineering: A Practitioner's Approach*, McGraw-Hill, New York.

Ramamoorthy, C., Garg, V. and Prakash, A. (1984) Programming in the large. *IEEE Transactions on Software Engineering*, **SE 12**, 769–783.

Rational Software (1998) Rational Unified Process Whitepaper: Best practices for software development teams, http://www.rational.com/products/whitepapers/100420.jsp

Raymond, E.S. (2001) *The Cathedral and the Bazaar: Musings on Linux and Open Source by an Accidental Revolutionary*, USA: O'Reilly.

Robey, D. and Markus, M. (1984) Rituals in information system design. *MIS Quarterly*, **March**, 5–15.

Rockart, J. and De Long, D. (1988) *Executive Support Systems*, Dow Jones-Irwin, Homewood, Illinois.

Ross, D. and Brackett, J. (1976) An approach to structured analysis. *Computer Decisions*, **September**, 40–44.

Royce, W. (1970) Managing the development of large software systems. *Proceedings of IEEE Wescon*.

Rumbaugh, J., Jacobson, I., Booch, G. (1999) *The Unified Modeling Language Reference Manual*, Addison Wesley Longman, Inc., Reading, MA.

Russo, N.L. and Wynekoop, J.L. (2000) System development methodologies: understanding the past and looking to the future, in *Proceedings of the 31st Annual Meeting of the Decision Sciences Institute*, Orlando, 677–679.

Russo, N.L., Kremer, A., and Brandt, I. (1999) Enterprise-wide software: factors affecting implementation and impacts on the IS function, in *Proceedings of the 30th Annual Meeting of the Decision Sciences Institute*, 1999, 808–810.

Russo, N. and Misic, M. (1998) Web applications: a whole new world of systems development? in M. Khosrowpour (ed.), *Effective Utilization and Management of Emerging Technologies: Proceedings of the Information Resources Management Association 1998 International Conference*, Idea Group Publishing, Hershey, PA, 843–844.

Russo, N., Wynekoop, J, and Walz, D. (1995) The use and adaptation of systems development methodologies, in Khosrowpour, M. (ed.), Managing Information & Communications in *a Changing Global Environment*, Idea Group Publishing, PA.

Sanden, B. (1985) *Systems Programming with JSP*, Studentlitteratur, Lund.

Schon, D. (1987) *Educating the Reflective Practitioner*, Jossey-Bass, San Franscisco.

Shomenta, J., Kamp, G., Hanso, B. and Simpson, B. (1983) Application approach worksheet: an evaluative tool for matching new development methods with appropriate applications, *MIS Quarterly*, **December**, pp. 1–10.

Sinha, M (1997) Development Practices at Microsoft, Seminar given at the Sixth International Conference on IS Development, Boise, Idaho, 11–14 August 1997.

Sommerville, I (1992), *Software Engineering*, Addison-Wesley Ltd, UK.

Stage, J. (1991) The use of descriptions in the analysis and design of information systems, In Stamper *et al.* (1991) *Collaborative Work, Social Communications and Information Systems*, North Holland, 237–260.

Stamper, R. (1988) Analysing the cultural aspect of a system. *International Journal of Information Management*, **8**, 3.

Stevens, W., Myers, G. and Constantine, L. (1974) Structured design. *IBM Systems Journal*, **13**, 2, 115–139.

Stevens, P. and Pooley, R. (2000) *Using UML: Software Engineering with Objects and Components*, Pearson Education Limited, Essex, England.

Stolterman, E. (1991). *Designarbetets dolda rationalitet – en studie av metodik och praktik inom systemutveckling*. (In English: The Hidden Rationality of Design Work – A study in the methodology and practice of system design). Doktorsavhandling (Ph.D. Thesis). Report UMADP-RRIPCS-14.91, Department of Informatics, Umeå University.

Stolterman, E. (1992). "How system designers think about design and methods". *Scandinavian Journal of Information Systems*, Vol. 4.

Storer, R. (1987) *Practical Program Development using JSP*, Blackwell Scientific Publications.

Sumner, M. and Sitek, J. (1986) Are structured methods for systems analysis and design being used? *Journal of Systems Management*, **June**, 18–23.

Tagg, R. (1983) Too many methodologies, in Baker, G. (ed.) *Data Analysis Update*, BCS Database Specialist Group.

Taylor, T, and Standish, T. (1982) Initial thoughts on rapid prototyping techniques, *ACM SIGSOFT Software Engineering Notes*, **7**, 5, 160–166.

Teichroew, D. and Sayani, H. (1971) Automation of system building. In Couger *et al.*, (1982) *Advanced System Development Feasibility Techniques*, Wiley & Sons, New York, 437–446.

Thomann, J. (1994) Data modelling in an OO world. *American Programmer*, **7**, 10, 44–53.

Tolvanen, Juha-Pekka (1998) *Incremental Method Engineering with Modeling Tools*, University of Jyvaskyla, Finland.

Torvalds, L. and Diamond, D. (2001) *Just for Fun: The Story of an Accidental Revolutionary*, Harper Collins, New York.

Verity, J. (1987) The OOPS revolution. *Datamation*, May 1, 73–78.

Verrijn-Stuart, A. (1989) Some reflections on the Namur conference on information system concepts, in Falkenberg, E. and Lindgreen, P. (eds) *Information System Concepts: An In-Depth Analysis*, IFIP, North Holland.

Vitalari, N. and Dickson, G. (1983) Problem solving for effective systems analysis: an experimental exploration. *Communications of the ACM*, **November**, 948–956.

Vonk, R. (1990) *Prototyping: The Effective Use of CASE Technology*, Prentice-Hall, London.

Ward, P. and Mellor, S. (1985) *Structured Development for Real-Time Systems*, Prentice-Hall, Englewood Cliffs.

Ward, P. (1989) How to integrate object-orientation with structured analysis and design. *IEEE Software*, **6**, 2, 74–82.

Ward, P. (1991) The evolution of structured analysis: Part I – the early years. American Programmer, **4**, 11, 4–16.

Ward, P. (1992a) The evolution of structured analysis: Part II – maturity and its problems. *American Programmer*, **5**, 4, 18–29.

Ward, P. (1992b) The evolution of structured analysis: Part III–spin-offs, mergers, and acquisitions. *American Programmer*, **5**, 9, 41–53.

Warnier, J. (1976) *Logical Construction of Programs*, Van Nostrand Reinhold, New York.

Weinberg, G. (1971) *The Psychology of Computer Programming*, Rheinhold, New York.

Welke, R. (1983) IS/DSS: DBMS support for information systems development, in Holsapple, C. and Whinston, A. (eds) *Database Management Systems*, Reidel, Dordrecht.

Williams, S. (2000) Open season: learning the ways of Mozilla, *Upside Today: The Tech Insider*, http://www.upside.com (12 Oct 2000).

Wilson, B. (1984) *Systems: Concepts, Methods and Applications*, Wiley, Maidenhead.

Wood-Harper, A., Antill, L. and Avison, D. (1985) *Information Systems Definition: The Multiview Approach*, Blackwell Scientific Publications, Oxford.

Yourdon, E. (1979) *Classics in Software Engineering*. Yourdon Press, New York.

Yourdon, E. (1988) Sayonara, structured stuff. *American Programmer*, **1**, 11, 40–49.

Yourdon, E. (1991) Sayonara, once again, structured stuff. *American Programmer*, **4**, 8, 31–38.

Yourdon, E. and Constantine, L. (1977) *Structured Design*, Yourdon Press, New York.

Zolnowski, J. and Ting, P. (1982) An insider's survey of software development, *Proc. 6th Int'l Conf. Software Engineering*, IEEE, Tokyo, Japan, 178–187.

Index